Talcott Parsons
and American Sociology

Talcott Parsons
and American
Sociology

Guy Rocher

Translated by **Barbara and Stephen Mennell**
with an introduction by **Stephen Mennell**

Nelson

Thomas Nelson and Sons Ltd
36 Park Street London W1Y 4DE

Nelson (Africa) Ltd
PO Box 18123 Nairobi Kenya

Thomas Nelson (Australia) Ltd
597 Little Collins Street Melbourne 3000

Thomas Nelson and Sons (Canada) Ltd
81 Curlew Drive Don Mills Ontario

Thomas Nelson (Nigeria) Ltd
PO Box 336 Apapa Lagos

First published in Great Britain by Thomas Nelson and Sons Ltd 1974

ISBN 017 712119 X

Printed in Great Britain by A. Wheaton & Company Exeter

Contents

Introduction

'What held me most transfixed was the Parsons problem'
George Homans[1]

For more than thirty years it has been impossible for sociologists to ignore the work of Talcott Parsons. In the decade and a half following the Second World War, Parsons and his followers dominated American sociology. If in recent years his work has attracted more hostile than sympathetic comment, it has remained very much at the centre of attention. Parsons, like only a few others since Marx, is a writer about whom almost every sociologist feels the need to form an opinion. The obstacles to an accurate understanding of his theories are, however, considerable. By its very nature, Parsons's writing is pitched at a very high level of abstraction—a level of abstraction which many commentators have felt unnecessary to the continuance of the discipline of sociology. It is also generally agreed that Parsons's prose style is often execrable, and abstractions clumsily expressed easily become obscurities. Abstraction and obscurity have been a cause of widespread irritation and exasperation. A third difficulty is that Parsons's writings are voluminous and widely scattered, and his theories have developed over time so that it is difficult to form an overall impression of his work and the intentions behind it.

Guy Rocher has now for the first time produced a comprehensible and careful survey of virtually the whole of Parsons's work from the beginning of his career right up to 1970. He discusses not only Parsons's strictly sociological theory and his political sociology, but also his personality theory and his views on the sociology of the economy, which are slightly less familiar to most sociologists. He shows, too, that the empirical essays, which have often been more admired than the theoretical statements, are an integral part of Parsons's work and have played a significant part in his theoretical

development. Rocher's book should make it much easier for
students of sociology to chart their way through Parsons's own
writings.

Though Professor Rocher's main aim is to provide a sympathetic
exegesis of Parsons's endeavours and achievements, he is by no
means uncritical. He shows that several of the more common
criticisms made of Parsons—that his theories have a built-in bias
towards conservatism, that they overemphasize equilibrium and
neglect change in society—are shallow and not founded on detailed
and unprejudiced reading of what Parsons actually says. At the
same time, in the course of his exposition, Rocher makes evident
several other potentially more important points of criticism. Despite
frequent references in his early work to what Whitehead called
the 'fallacy of misplaced concreteness', Parsons seems by no means
always to have avoided conceptual reification in his later work. He
also tends too often to proceed by means of ill-founded analogies.
As Rocher points out, the assumption of the theoretical unity of
micro- and macro-sociology—an assumption central to Parsons's
thought at least since 1953—rests on little more than insecure
analogies with Bales's research on small groups. Parsons takes it as
unproblematic that all systems of action, whether personality, social
or cultural systems and whatever their scale or scope, may be
treated as goal-directed. Such teleological accounts of supra-indi-
vidual aggregates are unacceptable to many sociologists. Three of
Parsons's leitmotivs—cybernetics, evolution and consensus on values
and goals—can be interpreted as attempts to make them more
acceptable. But, as Rocher again points out, the use Parsons makes
of cybernetics and evolutionary theory is also open to question.

Stepping back from the details of his theories, however, Parsons's
underlying intentions remain something of a puzzle. Rocher emphasizes that one of the abiding concerns of Parsons's career has been
the theoretical unification of the social sciences, and he very
successfully demonstrates how various aspects of Parsonian theory
have stemmed from this. Yet Homans[2] and others have argued that
Parsons's theories explain very little, that they are not for the most
part theories in the narrow sense at all. What, then, is the exact
status of the conceptual schemes, paradigms and taxonomies by
which Parsons has in large measure sought to unify social science?
Since Rocher's book was published in French, the most important

comment on Parsons's work to have appeared is Harold Bershady's examination of its epistemological foundations.[3] From the early years of his academic life, Bershady says, Parsons has been haunted by the problem of relativism—the view that absolutely certain and objective knowledge is, at least in the social sciences, impossible. Parsons's concern, therefore, has been not merely to establish *a* unifying conceptual scheme for social science, but *the* unifying scheme. In other words, Bershady argues, Parsons adopted an essentially neo-Kantian strategy, seeking to determine the immutable *a priori* categories of thought indispensable to any social scientific knowledge. Indeed, in *The Structure of Social Action*[4] Parsons compares his social action framework to the space–time categories of physics, which Kant saw as the fundamental forms of all perception. So far as I am aware, Parsons has never explicitly claimed to be a neo-Kantian, though in his essay on intellectual autobiography he mentions that he studied Kant thoroughly both as an undergraduate at Amherst and at Heidelberg under Jaspers.[5] At any rate, this interpretation of his strategy makes some sense out of his otherwise intriguing insistence that the pattern variables, the functional imperatives, the media of exchange and so on are 'logically exhaustive of all relevant possibilities' (even though the schemata themselves have tended to be modified over time as other relevant possibilities became apparent). It also makes sense of his efforts to pitch his schema at such a high level of abstraction that, as several writers have noted,[6] it is not irreconcilable with even so superficially dissimilar a perspective as Marxism. Furthermore, this interpretation suggests that Homans's charge that Parsons's 'theories' do not explain any particular phenomena is almost beside the point, for Parsons's concern is with form rather than content—with the basic forms or categories by which *all* social phenomena are known. As he digests Rocher's scholarly discussion, the reader will be able to make up his own mind whether Parsons has succeeded in establishing an unchallengeable triangulation point from which to map out the social world.

Among philosophers of science, the status of classificational schemata and other 'nontheoretic formulations' is still very problematic.[7] They cannot be directly tested empirically because, as such, they do not make propositions. One obvious measure of their validity is their usefulness when incorporated in true theories capable of empirical test. Even this is not simple, since sociology is relatively ill-provided with fully formalized theories. But using the test impressionistically, Parsons's conceptual schemata have not fared badly. Parsons's work does not by any means consist entirely of classifications and he has applied his concepts and paradigms to a great variety of empirical phenomena, producing 'explanation sketches' if not fully formalized explanations of many of them. And, as Rocher argues, Parsons's ideas have inspired a great deal of empirical research by others. Sociologists make extensive *ad hoc* use of bits of the Parsonian system, such as the pattern variables and the ideas of differentiation and integration. On the other hand, the AGIL schema has been much less popular, and very few sociologists are now Parsons's disciples to the extent of using his entire system in their work. If Parsons really did pursue the neo-Kantian objective of exposing the *a priori* categories of all social scientific thought, this partial success—the partial use of his system —must be a disappointment to him.

Parsons and the Parsonians are no longer so dominant in American sociology as they once were. Schools of thought have risen to prominence which are hostile to Parsons or at best treat his work with indifference. The 'radical sociology' associated with Mills, Horowitz, Gouldner and their followers, of which Rocher speaks in his last chapter, is only one of these schools. In some respects it is the least important. Certainly Gouldner has made some very shrewd criticisms of Parsons, but his culminating statement of them in *The Coming Crisis of Western Sociology*[8] was something of a disappointment. The particular criticisms were all there, but they were threaded together by an attempt to explain why Parsons said what he said by reference to his social background and academic milieu. Gouldner's book exemplifies Sir Karl Popper's fears about the sociology of knowledge serving as an intellectual cover for *ad hominem* attacks.[9]

Four other trends in American sociology during the 1960s and early 1970s deserve mention. The first of these might be called the symbolic interactionist renaissance. Symbolic interactionism (the name Herbert Blumer gave the theoretical outlook stemming particularly from George Herbert Mead) and the Chicago tradition never disappeared, but lay rather in a shadow during the Parsonian heyday of the late 1940s and 1950s. Rocher, I think, follows

Parsons in somewhat overstating the atheoretic empiricism of pre-war American sociology. Mead, Thomas and others had anticipated several aspects of Parsons's 'voluntaristic theory of action'[10] and this was the real cause of annoyance at his failure to mention any of the American writers in *The Structure of Social Action*. The Chicago sociologists were influenced by Mead and Thomas in particular. But it is certainly true that both before the war and since, sociologists in this tradition have usually chosen to have the moving parts of their theory less on public display than Parsons, who always leaves the engine cover open, lest anyone should ever mistake his sophisticated gas turbine for a twisted rubber band. At any rate, more than thirty years after his death in 1931, Mead's stock was still rising in American sociology. His influence on such notable writers as Erving Goffman and Howard S. Becker is clear.[11] The continuing activity and range of interactionist sociologists was demonstrated by the collection of their papers edited by the late Arnold Rose.[12]

A second and not dissimilar trend is social phenomenology. The key figure here was Alfred Schutz (1899–1959). In his native Austria, Schutz had been chiefly influenced by the work of Weber and Husserl, though after emigrating to America he absorbed many of the ideas of William James and G. H. Mead.[13] Schutz seems to have held Parsons's early work in some respect, though the carefree way in which Parsons later applied one conceptual scheme—the AGIL paradigm—to any and every system of action no matter what its scale and scope would surely have been unacceptable to Schutz.[14] One pair of Schutz's followers, Peter Berger and Thomas Luckmann, though not using any of Parsons's conceptual apparatus, nevertheless present a theory of social order not unlike Parsons's, stressing the significance of shared beliefs and outlooks.[15]

The other notable group who profess to be followers of Schutz, the ethnomethodologists, are very much more at odds with Parsons. Harold Garfinkel, usually acknowledged as the founder of this school of thought, is one of Parsons's own former students, and has paid tribute to Parsons's work 'for the penetrating depth and unfailing precision of its practical sociological reasoning on the constituent tasks of the problem of social order and its solutions'.[16] This compliment has struck many commentators as incongruous; Garfinkel (perhaps ironically) claims to see 'nothing to quarrel with' in more conventional forms of sociology,[17] but in fact he and his followers have found a good deal to quarrel with in the work of Parsons and many others. Their basic criticism is that 'the earmark of practical sociological reasoning, wherever it occurs, is that it seeks to remedy the indexical properties of members' talk and conduct'.[18] By this they mean that the conceptual schemes of conventional sociology, of which Parsons's is the most ambitious, are used to impose sociologists' mental models on those of their subjects. For their own part, ethnomethodologists have been influenced not only by Schutz but also by Wittgensteinian philosophy. There is a loose resemblance between Parsons's emphasis on the normative element in social life and the Wittgensteinian conception of rule-governed linguistic behaviour. But the similarity does not go much further than that. As Bershady shows, Parsons has always seen causal explanations more or less of the 'covering law' variety as an ideal for sociology.[19] The ethnomethodologists are out of sympathy with this fundamental endeavour. They are suspicious of sociologists' use of their concepts to generalize about many particular situations. Rocher mentions that many pre-war American sociologists viewed all generalization with suspicion. If so, then in this respect if no other the ethnomethodologists are in an authentic American tradition.

Finally, in a less radical way, many other American sociologists have turned away from theory in Parsons's grand manner to pursue empirical research by increasingly sophisticated methods. There has perhaps been some return to what Rocher sees as the pre-war pattern of American sociology. If the new empiricists have a hero in the older generation, it is not Talcott Parsons but Paul Lazarsfeld. The growth of mathematical sociology in the last decade, associated with such names as James S. Coleman, Hubert M. Blalock Jr, and Harrison White,[20] is particularly noteworthy. But I do not believe theirs is an atheoretic empiricism; it is merely that the theories they now seek are mainly of Merton's middle-range type, which many would see as the only true theories sociology possesses. And it is certainly striking that Blalock's use of multiple regression to establish causal explanations, and Coleman's work on the theory of collective action, make much more substantive use of the methods of economic analysis than do Parsons's economic analogies.

Yet I think it will be apparent to the reader of Rocher's book that Parsons's work continues to merit study. It is packed with insights, and in it are raised all the main theoretical and philosophical problems of contemporary sociology. Even if eventually one rejects Parsons's solutions, to study his ideas is an effective way of establishing one's intellectual bearings—even though one may in the end side with his critics.

In our translation of Professor Rocher's French text, we have somewhat filled out references to Parsons's own works. Difficult as they may often be, they are more accessible to English readers than French, and at points it is useful to know on exactly which passage Rocher is basing his remarks. In a few places we have gone directly to Parsons or quoted or paraphrased his words rather than translating M. Rocher's paraphrase. Our only omissions are minor ones —repetitions and references to French sources and terminology which we judged would only be confusing to the English reader. Notes marked with my initials (SJM) are of course mine and not Rocher's.

As translators we should particularly like to thank Patricia Chandrasekera for occasionally giving us the kind of help which only a native French speaker can easily provide. Herminio Martins of St Antony's College, Oxford, made some extremely useful comments on Rocher's book and on an early draft of part of the translation. Professor Parsons himself kindly supplied the up-to-date bibliography of his writings given in Appendix I. We are grateful, too, to Mary O'Rourke for so willingly typing the manuscript.

STEPHEN MENNELL
Exeter, January 1974.

NOTES

1. G. C. Homans, *Sentiments and Activities* (London, Routledge and Kegan Paul, 1962) p 43.
2. G. C. Homans, 'Bringing Men Back In', *American Sociological Review*, **29** 6, 1964, pp 809–18; 'Contemporary Theory in Sociology', in *A Handbook of Modern Sociology*, edited by R. E. L. Faris (Chicago, Rand McNally, 1964); *The Nature of Social Science* (New York, Harcourt Brace and World, 1967).

3. Harold J. Bershady, *Ideology and Social Knowledge* (Oxford, Basil Blackwell, 1973).
4. Talcott Parsons, *The Structure of Social Action* (New York, McGraw-Hill, 1937) p 732ff.
5. Talcott Parsons, 'On Building Social System Theory: A Personal History', *Daedalus*, **99** 4, 1970, pp 826, 876 (note 10), 881 (note 68).
6. See for example P. L. van den Berghe, 'Dialectic and Functionalism: Toward a Theoretical Synthesis', *American Sociological Review*, **28** 5, 1963, pp 695–705.
7. See the excellent discussion in R. S. Rudner, *Philosophy of Social Science* (Englewood Cliffs, NJ, Prentice-Hall, 1966) chapter 2. Rudner and most other philosophers of science, incidentally, are now very far from taking 'the positivistic view of the total cultural self-sufficiency of science' of which Parsons speaks ('On Building Social System Theory', *op cit*, p 881, note 73).
8. Alvin W. Gouldner, *The Coming Crisis of Western Sociology* (New York, Basic Books, 1970).
9. K. R. Popper, *The Open Society and Its Enemies* (London, Routledge and Kegan Paul, 4th ed, 1962) vol 2, chapter 23.
10. Roscoe C. Hinkle, 'Antecedents of the Action Orientation in American Sociology before 1935', *American Sociological Review*, **28** 5, 1963, pp 705–15.
11. See, *inter alia*, Erving Goffman, *The Presentation of Self in Everyday Life* (New York, Doubleday, 1959) and *Asylums* (Garden City, NY, Doubleday, 1961); Howard S. Becker, *Outsiders* (New York, Free Press, 1963).
12. Arnold M. Rose (ed), *Human Behaviour and Social Processes* (Boston, Houghton Mifflin, 1962).
13. Alfred Schutz, *The Phenomenology of the Social World*, translated by G. Walsh and F. Lehnert (Evanston, Ill., Northwestern University Press, 1967); *Collected Papers*, 3 vols (The Hague, Martinus Nijhoff, 1962–6).
14. This tactic represents what Helmut Wagner has called 'the fallacy of displacement of scope', in his article 'Displacement of Scope: A Problem of the Relationship between Small-scale and Large-scale Sociological Theories', *American Journal of Sociology*, **69** 6, 1964, pp 571–84.
15. P. Berger and T. Luckmann, *The Social Construction of Reality* (London, Allen Lane, 1967); P. Berger, *The Social Reality of Religion* (Harmondsworth, Penguin, 1971) [originally published as *The Sacred Canopy* (Garden City, NY, Doubleday, 1967)].
16. Harold Garfinkel, *Studies in Ethnomethodology* (Englewood Cliffs, NJ, Prentice-Hall, 1967) p ix. Other works by ethnomethodologists include A. V. Cicourel, *Method and Measurement in Sociology* (New York, Free Press, 1964) and *Cognitive Sociology* (Harmondsworth, Penguin, 1973); Jack D. Douglas (ed), *Understanding Everyday Life* (London, Routledge and Kegan Paul, 1971); P. Filmer, *et al*, *New Directions in Sociological Theory* (London, Collier-Macmillan, 1972). Filmer discusses Garfinkel's attitude to Parsons on pp 218–22.
17. Garfinkel, *op cit*, p viii.
18. *ibid*, pp 10–11.
19. Bershady, *op cit*, p 48. For a typical Wittgensteinian onslaught at the 'covering law' model of explanation (which is associated with Hempel

and other philosophers of science of similar persuasion) see A. R. Louch, *Explanation and Human Action* (Oxford, Basil Blackwell, 1966).

20. James S. Coleman, *Introduction to Mathematical Sociology* (New York, Free Press, 1964) and *The Mathematics of Collective Action* (Chicago, Aldine, 1973); Hubert M. Blalock Jr, *Causal Inferences in Non-experimental Research* (Chapel Hill, University of North Carolina Press, 1964) and *Toward a Theory of Minority Group Relations* (New York, John Wiley, 1967); Harrison C. White, *Anatomy of Kinship: Mathematical Models for Structures of Cumulated Roles* (Englewood Cliffs, NJ, Prentice-Hall, 1963), and *Chains of Opportunity: System Models of Mobility in Organizations* (Cambridge, Mass., Harvard University Press, 1970).

I. American Sociology's 'Incurable Theorist'

Talcott Parsons, in dedicating his book *The Social System* to his wife, described himself as an 'incurable theorist'. It would be difficult to find two words which better defined this man's career and the role he has played in American sociology for the last forty years. Talcott Parsons occupies a special and conspicuous place among American sociologists. Until he came on the scene, American sociology had been dominated by empiricism, and was in some danger of sinking into a quagmire of detailed and local studies. Parsons brought about a theoretical revolution. His entire work is directed towards a single objective : the development of a conceptual and theoretical framework intended to give sociology truly scientific status, and at the same time to relate it logically to the other social sciences. This one underlying purpose gives Parsons's writings a unity which at first glance they may seem to lack.

It is something of a paradox that out of the prevailing empiricism of American sociology should have sprung the most abstract theorist in contemporary social science. Parsons is by no means typical of American sociology. With his formidably theoretical approach, the high level of generality at which he works, and the difficult language he uses, Parsons swam against the stream of almost all American sociology, which he has continually nettled and offended. His work has met with widespread opposition, vigorous criticism and persistent resistance in American sociological circles.

But, at the same time, Parsons's sociology is closely bound up with America and American sociology. American society has given Parsons much food for thought and served as his principal research laboratory—to such an extent that some critics of Parsonian sociology have seen it as no more than a pseudo-expert formulation of American ideology. Moreover, Parsons has influenced several generations of American sociologists; more than anyone else he founded a school of thought, and amongst those he has influenced can be counted many of the leading figures of contemporary American sociology, such as Robert K. Merton, Robin Williams, Neil Smelser, Edward Shils, Robert Bellah and many others.

Talcott Parsons's sociology, then, presents something of a contradiction. It belongs to American sociology, but for a long time represented a foreign body within it. It has been very influential yet very much criticized. It is pitched at the highest level of abstraction, yet is accused of reflecting American society and ideology.

To understand why Parsons's work was found surprising, incomprehensible and even offensive in the United States, particularly when it first appeared, it is essential to describe the prevailing climate of American sociology between the wars. We shall then be better able to appreciate how far Parsons's thought represented something bold and innovative. But let us first say who Parsons is and briefly outline his career and the main phases of his work.[1]

1.1 An Exclusively Academic Career

Talcott Parsons was born in 1902, at Colorado Springs in the State of Colorado. His father was a minister in the Congregational church and took an active part in the Protestant campaign for social reform known as the Social Gospel movement. He also taught English at Colorado College, where he became Dean, before being finally appointed President of Marietta College in Ohio. The young Parsons thus grew up in a Protestant atmosphere, in the puritan and reformist tradition of the American Midwest in the first quarter of the century. At the same time, he experienced the severely austere and socially involved intellectual climate of the small American colleges of that period.

From 1920 to 1924, Parsons was at Amherst College, where he at first concentrated on biology and philosophy, intending either to do graduate work in biology or, following the example of an elder brother, to go into medicine. It was in the course of his third year at Amherst that he began to take an interest in the social sciences, and he finally decided to pursue postgraduate studies in sociology. Parsons himself recognizes that his father's social reformism was not unconnected with this reorientation : the family atmosphere

had disposed him to feel attracted to the work of the 'institutionalist' economists, who sought to break out of the excessively
narrow framework of classical economics to study the institutional
aspects of economic phenomena and their relation to the wider
social structure. The very origins of Parsons's vocation for sociology
illustrate once more the long-established link between American
sociology and Protestant social reformism.

Nevertheless, Parsons was not much attracted towards the pro-
grammes of study that American universities offered in sociology,
which were too exclusively empirical. Feeling himself drawn more
towards European universities, after obtaining his BA he took
advantage of an uncle's financial assistance to spend a year at the
London School of Economics. There he studied with the sociologists
Hobhouse and Ginsberg, the historian Tawney, the political theorist
Laski, and particularly with the anthropologist Malinowski, who
came to have a marked influence on him. At the end of this year
in London, he obtained a scholarship to study at the University
of Heidelberg (1925–6) where he went with no more specific purpose than of benefiting from the intellectual atmosphere of one of
the German universities, which then had a very great reputation
and influence in American academic circles. It was there that his
vocation for social science was confirmed, under the decisive
influence of a man whose prestige was continually growing in
Germany : Max Weber. Weber had already been dead for five
years when Parsons came to Heidelberg, but his presence was still
very much felt there. His widow, Marianne Weber, fostered this by
holding a 'salon' each Sunday afternoon, which the young Parsons
frequented. In Max Weber's work Parsons found the elements of
an analytic framework which seemed to him to be gravely lacking
in sociology; an interpretation of the historic role of Protestantism
in comparison with the other great religions; and an explanation
of contemporary capitalism, of which the United States had become
a kind of archetype.

At Amherst College, the institutionalist economists had drawn
Parsons's attention to the complexity of the relations between
economic structures and social and political structures. Reading
Max Weber, in whose work he found an exploration of the same
problems, but extended to much greater historical perspectives,
revived his interest in the study of economic institutions. Having to

write a thesis to obtain his doctorate at the University of Heidelberg, Parsons chose to make a comparative analysis of the idea of capitalism as a socio-economic institution, in the writings of Karl Marx, Werner Sombart and Max Weber. This thesis was never published, but Parsons drew from it his first article, which appeared in the United States in the *Journal of Political Economy*.[2]

On his return to the United States, Parsons first spent a year at Amherst College, as Instructor in economics. Then, in 1927, he moved to Harvard University, where he was to spend the rest of his career in teaching and research. Compared with the majority of American academics, who move readily from one university to another, Parsons's permanence at Harvard proved highly unusual. However, his debut there was not very encouraging; he had to wait several years before achieving the status of professor and permanent 'tenure'.

He went to Harvard as an Instructor in the Department of Economics, a post he held from 1927 to 1931. As he himself explains, unlike American qualifications, his Heidelberg doctorate was not specifically in any one social scientific discipline—which allowed him to teach economics as well as sociology. It was during this period that Parsons translated Max Weber's *The Protestant Ethic and the Spirit of Capitalism* into English; he also took advantage of this stay among economists to augment his knowledge of economics, under the guidance of teachers like F. W. Taussig, T. N. Carver, Edwin F. Gay and Joseph Schumpeter.

In 1931, Parsons moved to the Department of Sociology, which had just been created under Pitirim Sorokin. He retained the title of plain Instructor, which still placed him at the bottom of the academic ladder at Harvard. Not until 1936 was he appointed Assistant Professor, and only in 1939—two years after the publication of his important work *The Structure of Social Action*—did he first attain a tenured rank as Associate Professor.

Parsons's university career was almost unaffected by the war—unlike many academics at Harvard and other American universities, who were called up into the services or recruited into government posts. Parsons did, however, do some teaching in the School for Overseas Administration, and acted as consultant to the Foreign Economic Administration, advising on the policies the United States should adopt towards Germany after the war.

In 1944, Parsons thought seriously about leaving Harvard University. It was partly to keep him there that he was offered the chairmanship of the Department of Sociology. In this new position, Parsons was at the centre of an important reorganization of the teaching of the social sciences. Together with the social psychologist Gordon Allport, the clinical psychologist Henry Murray, the anthropologist Clyde Kluckhohn and the sociologists George Homans and Samuel Stouffer, he formed the Department of Social Relations, the aim of which was to rearrange and integrate the teaching of the social sciences within the same multi-disciplinary structure.[3] The new Department of Social Relations was set up in 1946, and Parsons was its Chairman until 1956. It is interesting that Parsons sought to bring about in academic institutions the unification of the social sciences which has, as we shall see, been the main thrust of his theoretical enterprise. There is a congruity between Parsons's theoretical interests and his activity as a teacher and administrator which has never been adequately recognized.

To his already heavy academic duties, Parsons added several others outside the University. First, he was elected President of the Eastern Sociological Society for the year 1942. In 1949 he was elected President of the American Sociological Association, at a time when it was rapidly expanding and required its President to devote a large part of his time to it. Since then, Parsons has always remained active in various roles in the American Sociological Association. In particular, he was the first editor of *The American Sociologist*, the Association's 'house organ' which deals with matters of concern to the sociological profession.

Parsons has also been active in the American Association of University Professors and particularly in the American Academy of Arts and Sciences, of which he was President in 1967—the first social scientist to hold this office. The Academy publishes the journal *Daedalus*, in which several important articles by Parsons have appeared.

Finally, Parsons was among the first American sociologists to make contact with Soviet sociology. In fact in 1964 he was the first to go to the USSR at the invitation of the Soviet Academy of Sciences to give a series of lectures on American sociology.[4]

1.2 The Development of Parsons's Work

Such a full university career has not, however, prevented Parsons publishing a vast amount. His whole life has been dedicated to his work, an outline of which will now be given before undertaking a more detailed study in later chapters.

Without too great an oversimplification, three stages can be distinguished in the development of Parsons's work and thought. In the first, Parsons unravelled the main themes of what he called a theory of social action from the work of several of the major precursors of contemporary sociology, notably Weber, Durkheim and Pareto. During the second stage, Parsons was occupied in systematizing this theory of social action, in spelling out its logical and scientific foundations, and in broadening it into a general theory of human action. In the third period, Parsons set out to apply this general theory of action to several different social sciences : economics, psychology and political science. This led him to amend, but mainly to extend, his general theory, finally giving it an evolutionary twist. The latter led Parsons back, in a rather unforeseen way, to the great historical panoramas of Comte, Spencer and Sorokin.

Let us now look in more detail at each of these stages. The first resulted in the volume *The Structure of Social Action*, on which Parsons worked for many years. It is known that the design of this work only gradually took shape for its author. He could be said to have begun work on it at Heidelberg, when he discovered the work of Max Weber. It was there that he first became acquainted with the idea of social action as used by Weber, and where he saw that this notion might be the theoretical link between economics and sociology.

Then, at Harvard, Parsons turned his attention to the English economist Alfred Marshall, with the intention of uncovering the psychological and social bases on which the major theorist of classical economics had formed his conception of the motivation of human action and economic activity. This led him to draw attention to the inadequacies of any psychology and sociology based too simply on liberal and utilitarian ideology.[5]

Parsons next looked to Pareto and Durkheim to correct and supplement Marshall's model of economic behaviour. Parsons was introduced to Pareto's work by Lawrence Henderson, a professor of physiology at Harvard who had become the leading American interpreter of the Italian economist and sociologist,[6] and who influenced Parsons quite strongly. Unlike Marshall, Pareto had developed a detailed analysis of non-rational action, which the classical economists had excluded from their universe of discourse. Parsons saw this as an important contribution to the theory of human action. Besides, it was from Pareto and Henderson that Parsons learned to consider human action, non-rational as well as rational, as a system, and he became convinced that this idea was indispensable to all truly scientific analysis.[7]

As for Durkheim, much of what Parsons had been taught, especially by Ginsberg and Malinowski, was positively misleading, and as he wrote, 'much unlearning of what was not true about Durkheim became necessary'.[8] In English-speaking sociological circles, Durkheim was then taken to have invented and hypostatized a kind of 'collective consciousness' (that was how the idea of *conscience collective* was translated into English) which animated society. This led to Durkheim being accused of the 'group mind fallacy' and seen as a dangerous nominalist. To his great surprise, Parsons discovered a completely different Durkheim. The idea of the *conscience collective*, far from being what he had been led to expect, seemed to him rather to be the key to the social psychological explanation of moral conduct and of normative social action. In the economic sphere, the role Durkheim attributed to contract seemed to him to cast new light on the functioning of modern economic institutions. Finally, it was in Durkheim that Parsons learned to follow the contrary and complementary interplay of the forces of social solidarity and disorganization, and of differentiation and integration.[9]

This was how Talcott Parsons put together his first great work, *The Structure of Social Action*, which appeared in 1937 and rapidly confirmed Parsons's reputation as a theorist. In this voluminous study, Parsons reorganized his analyses of Marshall, Weber, Pareto and Durkheim with three rather different purposes in mind at once. His first objective was to look, one after the other, at the explanations each had given of modern capitalism, its origins and development. In this respect, Parsons was continuing the research he had begun in his doctoral thesis. There was one important difference, however. In his thesis, Parsons set out from the Marxist analysis of capitalism and compared it with that of Sombart and Weber. In 1937, Marx occupied a much more modest and even secondary position in his work.

On a higher level of generality, the second objective of the book was to compare the ways in which Marshall, Pareto, Weber and Durkheim resolved the problem of the relations between economic activity and the wider social context. In Parsons's view, this second objective was closely connected with the first; for Parsons, capitalism had to be explained and analysed as an economic *institution*— as a structure of property and production closely dependent on social structures, values, attitudes and non-economic behaviour. Parsons was convinced that the wholly economic explanation of capitalism, and more generally of any economic structure, was inadequate without the contribution of sociological explanations. He had forcefully expressed this conviction in the first articles he published between 1928 and 1937. In *The Structure of Social Action*, he pursued this issue further through his discussion of his chosen authors. It will be seen later that this problem is one of the main themes which give some unity to Parsons's theoretical work.

The third and most prominent and explicit objective was to reveal a 'convergence', concealed in the thought of these four writers, towards what Parsons called a 'voluntaristic theory of action'. On the one hand, according to Parsons, each of these authors in his own way rejected positivism,[10] and asserted the role in human action of 'subjectivity'—a person's motives, the goals he selects and pursues, and the values to which he adheres. On the other hand, these four writers also went beyond purely utilitarian analysis in showing, each once more in his own way, that the pursuit of personal interest is not the only, nor even the dominant motive behind human action. Man defines and adheres to norms, values and goals, which he takes as rules of conduct. Thus the old problem of the rationality of human action and of the relationship between means and ends—which was central to the utilitarian theory—was recast in a new form, and this appeared much more promising to Parsons.

The Structure of Social Action is perhaps the most frequently cited of Parsons's works, no doubt because of the breadth and richness of his analysis of the development of Western social thought. Certainly this remains Parsons's *magnum opus*, his most valuable if not his most original contribution to sociological theory. But for Parsons himself, this was only a beginning—a very important one no doubt, but incomplete. For at the end of this work he set himself the task of elaborating this 'theory of action', the elements of which he had discerned in the writings of his predecessors. He set out to explore the numerous avenues that they had opened up or merely pointed out, and to build on the foundations they had laid.

The second period of Parsons's work began after the publication of *The Structure of Social Action*. He now set out to solve the theoretical problems he had posed, trying to make his hypotheses more precise and to put them to test. This led him to publish a series of essays over several years dealing with a variety of subjects : the organization of the family, religion, the professions, social stratification, political movements and economic motivation. Essays and studies on particular topics have been very important in the development of Parsons's thought, as we shall see in more detail later. At any rate, Parsons's theoretical work did not appear in book form at this period, but was rather scattered throughout a large numbers of articles, on empirical as well as theoretical topics.

During the period from 1937 to about 1950, Parsons published some thirty articles in which he can be seen exploring various ways forward. He was trying to assemble the parts of a general theory which he had glimpsed, but which still needed systematizing. At the beginning of the 1950s these efforts finally came to fruition. In 1951 and 1953 Parsons published three volumes which marked a turning point in his work, for it was then that he first brought together the fundamental elements of his general theory in a definitive way. These three works, *Toward a General Theory of Action*, with Edward A. Shils, Clyde Kluckhohn and others (1951), *The Social System* (1951) and *Working Papers in the Theory of Action*, with Robert F. Bales and Edward A. Shils (1953), have to be read together because they complement each other.

Three main things can be said about Parsons's work at this stage. First, he began to realize the enormous scope of the general theory of action; it had to be sufficiently general and abstract to be applicable to all forms of human action, not just to economic action or social action in the narrow sense. Second, Parsons defined in more detail his model of what he called a system of action; his approach became systemic rather than structural–functionalist. He came to consider functionalism to be only one form of systems analysis, which is something much wider. Third, Parsons laid the foundations of his systemic analysis of action with the 'pattern variables' and the four functional dimensions of all systems of action.

Since sociology appeared to Parsons to be one particular discipline within the framework of the general theory of action, it remained for him to show that the general theory could also be applied to other spheres of human action. It was this which was principally to occupy the third stage of Parsons's work and led him into fields far removed from sociology. Collaborating with Neil Smelser, Parsons applied his model to the analysis of the economic system in *Economy and Society*, published in 1956. This laid the foundations of what he reckoned to be a new economic sociology and added important new items to his conceptual armoury. From his earliest studies in economics, Parsons had been much impressed by its progress in constructing analytic theories and establishing a clear definition of what constituted its main theoretical problems. He was convinced that its techniques of analysis could be adapted to all other forms of social action. In particular, economic analysis was the pattern on which Parsons based his model of interaction between systems and sub-systems, and the media of exchange which facilitate this interaction.

At the same time as he was exploring economic territory, Parsons was doing the same thing in other fields of social action, notably in psychology and political science. In the early 1940s Parsons was introduced to psycho-analysis; he read Freud thoroughly and even underwent a didactic analysis. Although not medically qualified, he was admitted as a special candidate to the Boston Psycho-analytic Institute. Freud then became a dominant influence in the development of Parsons's thought. Parsons particularly sought to build a bridge between Freudian psycho-analytic theory and the general theory of action he was developing. To this end he wrote a series of articles on personality structure, learning, socialization, education, and the relationship between the personality and social environment. Most of these articles have been reprinted in *Family,*

Socialization, and Interaction Process (1955) and in *Social Structure and Personality* (1964).

In political science, as in economics, Parsons took a keen interest from the start of his career, inspired in this particularly by Max Weber. After 1960 he returned intensively to this field. Before that Parsons had sought to explain particular political phenomena which perplexed him, such as Nazism, fascism, McCarthyism and political propaganda. But after 1960, he tried to integrate political science into his general theory of action. He did this by borrowing the model he had developed in *Economy and Society* and applying it to political processes. Parsons's political sociology, scattered through a large number of articles published over a period of more than thirty years, in the end adds up to an impressive achievement. The most important of these essays are collected in *Politics and Social Structure* (1969).

Finally, Parsons set out to round off his work by formulating an interpretation of the general evolution of societies and civilizations. Strongly influenced by nineteenth-century evolutionism and especially by Herbert Spencer, Parsons in his turn has attempted to define the successive stages through which societies evolve. This is found in the two small books *Societies: Evolutionary and Comparative Perspectives* (1966) and *The System of Modern Societies* (1971).

This brief survey gives only a bird's eye view of Parsons's writings as a whole. If we are fully to understand his intentions, the theory he has developed, and the many avenues of research he has explored, we shall have to return to each of his various works. But first we must set Parsons more fully in the context of American sociology.

1.3 American Sociology Between the Wars

From his very first articles, and still more after *The Structure of Social Action*, Talcott Parsons's intellectual personality stood out in the landscape of the American sociology of the period. In many respects, Parsons broke with the sociological traditions of his country; the theory he outlined in that book opened up new vistas and was much discussed.

The dominant feature of American sociology between the wars was its empiricism—not a theoretical or radical empiricism, but a factual empiricism, practised with a kind of élan and enthusiasm which left little room for doubt. There was a very strong prejudice in favour of empirical research, consisting of a kind of veneration for 'facts', neither distorted nor disguised by any conceptual framework or theoretical preconceptions. Theory was often equated with philosophy, with political ideologies, or with what was scornfully labelled 'metaphysics', and it seemed strangely antithetical to scientific research.

The empirical work of American sociology in this period is associated with two traditions: the 'Chicago School', and the series of great monographs on small towns and communities produced by sociologists outside Chicago. From the beginning of the twentieth century, the University of Chicago had been the most dynamic centre of sociological teaching and research. The Department of Sociology at Chicago gave a great impetus to research and imbued its staff, students and associates with a strongly empirical bent, so that they can be described as a real school of sociology. But in fact it was a very loose school of thought since, strictly speaking, it never had any theory or common doctrine. What united the members of the Chicago school, or at least allowed them to identify with each other, was first their trust in sociological research and their constant endeavour to apply the most rigorous methods available to a great variety of topics. Another thing they had in common was their favourite laboratory—the urban environment. Under the leadership particularly of Park and Burgess, whose names are associated both with the Chicago school and American urban sociology,[11] research was carried out not only in great American cities like Chicago, but in medium sized and small towns. And they were especially interested in conflict and the pathological aspects of the urban milieu. The problems of ethnic groups and race relations were extensively discussed in the 1920s and 1930s by such writers as Park, Thomas, Wirth, Frazier and Hughes.[12] Important studies were made of various effects of—as it was supposed—social disorganization, including those of Sutherland on crime in general and 'white-collar crime' in particular, Thrasher on delinquent gangs, Faris and Dunham on mental illness, Shaw and McKay on juvenile delinquency.[13] The Chicago school also introduced more refined research techniques. At first, Park and Burgess preferred ethnographic techniques in the style of W. I. Thomas. Later, W. F. Ogburn powerfully advocated quantitative methods, and through his influence the Chicago department became the most advanced in this sphere.

The second tradition of empirical research was that associated with the great series of community studies. These had a strong and lasting influence on American sociology, and a great deal of research effort was put into this kind of study. The biggest of them, and still the most celebrated was that undertaken by W. Lloyd Warner in a small coastal town in New England. The account of this project, which was begun in 1930 and lasted several years, ran to five volumes.[14] Several other studies deserve mention, especially those by Robert and Helen Lynd of Muncie, Indiana,[15] by Allison Davis, Burleigh and Mary Gardner of a town in the South,[16] by James West of one in the Mid-West,[17] and by William Foote Whyte on the Italian quarter in Boston.[18]

In their monographs, these writers refrained from representing life in one town as typical of the whole of American life. However, in the absence of any more macroscopic studies, there remained a strong temptation to think of these monographs as representative of the American way of life. This made them very successful and celebrated. Their most notable contribution to American sociology perhaps lay in the fact that they produced evidence of the existence of more clearly defined social classes than Americans readily credited at the time, and even a genuine caste system dividing Blacks and Whites in the Deep South.

It is probably due to the influence of these thoroughly researched local studies that American sociologists for a long time refused to write or talk about American society as a whole, still less of Western society. Reared in a tradition of empiricism and detailed monographs, they viewed all generalization with considerable suspicion. They tended to assume that to go beyond directly observable and demonstrable realities was to revive what they pejoratively labelled 'impressionism', and that that could only mislead their readers and bring sociology into disrepute. So, concerned for precision and methodological rigour, American sociologists had for some time accepted that they could have only detailed and segmentary views of society.

As a matter of fact, it was in an area contiguous to sociology, in social psychology, that American sociologists had made a positive theoretical contribution. As Parsons himself observed 'up to the middle of the present century at least, the "social psychology" associated with the concept of "symbolic interaction" has probably constituted the most important distinctively American contribution to sociological theory'.[19] Prominent early members of the school which subsequently became known as symbolic interactionism included W. I. Thomas, C. H. Cooley and George Herbert Mead.[20] These three theorists contributed greatly to the analysis of interpersonal relations. One of their key concepts was that of the 'self', and they stressed the significance of perception both of the self and others. These perceptions both shape and are shaped by the process of interaction. More generally, they pointed to the influence of the immediate social environment on the individual personality. Thus, alongside an empiricist sociology which produced no theoretical framework, social psychology was making notable progress. Its development was assisted both by advances in individual psychology at that time and by the prevailing Protestant climate in the United States, which favoured an individualistic rather than collectivist interpretation of social phenomena.

In this perspective, it is not surprising that American sociologists thought more highly of Gabriel Tarde than Emile Durkheim. We have already mentioned the prejudices which then existed in the United States concerning Durkheim. In contrast, they were strongly influenced by Gabriel Tarde's social psychology, his discussion of imitation, and his theory of society. Tarde defined society as a complex of interpersonal relationships between individuals and groups which reciprocally influenced each other. Among German sociologists, it was Georg Simmel in particular who influenced the Chicago school and American sociology generally at the beginning of the century. From 1896, mainly under the auspices of Albion W. Small, one of the pioneers of American sociology, Simmel's articles were regularly published in the *American Journal of Sociology*.[21] The American tradition of studies of interaction in dyads, triads and small groups, and of work on the theoretical foundations of interaction, stems in large part from Simmel's influence.

Another feature of American sociology in this period, again linked to its empiricism, was the almost total absence of interest in the history of sociology and social thought. American sociologists believed above all in empirical research, which little by little would bring more precise knowledge of specific areas of society. The rest was regarded as a kind of superfluous culture, which the whole American teaching profession of that period treated with suspicion. They preferred to see the student of sociology read and absorb the recently published monographs rather than the writings of the founding fathers, such as Comte, Marx, Spencer and Durkheim, whom they considered to be more philosophical than scientific, and more dangerously dogmatic than illuminating.

1.4 Against the Tide of American Sociology

Such, briefly summarized, were some of the chief features of the intellectual climate in American sociology between the wars. Parsons, rather more inclined towards abstractions than empirical inquiry, was passionately interested in the history of ideas, and very soon became conspicuous among his sociological colleagues. One way in which Parsons's originality was apparent from his earliest publications was that he was at first inspired exclusively by European thinkers who were little, or at best inaccurately, known in the United States. Parsons was largely responsible for making Max Weber's ideas known to Americans; he was the first to translate Weber's work and one of the first to comment upon it in English. Equally, he contributed more than anyone else to the rehabilitation of Emile Durkheim in the United States. As for Vilfredo Pareto, he presented and analysed his work with a clarity and mastery which have scarcely been equalled since.[22] In his economic research, Parsons turned to the English economist Alfred Marshall, whom he regarded as the principal theorist of modern economics, and whose work also lent itself best to a sociological discussion. Of the works of Marx and the socialists, it is difficult to say exactly what Parsons read, but it is clear that he knew some of Marx's work fairly well, because he refers to it frequently in his first articles and in *The Structure of Social Action.* Today it is hard to appreciate how unorthodox it then was for an American sociologist to read and discuss Marx.

The other writers to whom Parsons refers in his early work are Tönnies, Simmel, Mauss, Halbwachs, Piaget, Malthus and

Malinowski. For a long time he was not forgiven for having made no reference to any American sociologist in *The Structure of Social Action*. Not until after this work did Parsons begin to mention the contribution to contemporary sociology of Cooley, Thomas and Mead, in whose works he became more and more interested. But the names of these three writers do not even appear in the index of *The Structure of Social Action*.[23]

Parsons's first image was as a sociologist whose intellectual origins were exclusively European. In Europe they were not only German, as were those of many American intellectuals of the period, but also French, English and Italian. From the very start, Parsons placed himself directly in the great stream of social thought of the last two centuries. Beyond the first sociologists and immediate fore-runners of sociology, Parsons was linked mainly to the tradition of thought of the English philosophers, Hobbes, Locke and Mill. In opposition to these he placed, on the one hand, the German idealist and historicist tradition from Hegel through Dilthey and Sombart to Weber, and, on the other hand, the positivism of Comte, Marx and Spencer. The influence on his thought of Hobbes and the English philosophers was particularly great. It was largely in their terms that he posed the problems of the persistence of society, of the bases of social life, of the essential structure of human action, and of the forces promoting solidarity, integration and change in society.

These intellectual preoccupations were the basis of the anti-empiricism which, perhaps more than anything else, distinguished Parsons from other American sociologists at this period. At the level of philosophy of science, Parsons can be said to be downright anti-empiricist. Not that he despises empirical research in itself; he respects his colleagues for their methodological refinements, their rigorous and precise techniques. Though he himself admits to being little versed in research methods, he has never intended to criticize or scoff—as others have done—at those who devote attention to polishing their research techniques. On the contrary Parsons has often paid tribute to them, and has himself at various times under-taken empirical research.

The point Parsons was making was something quite different. He was convinced that the requirements of science were not met by empirical research alone. Empirical findings needed to be fitted into a theoretical framework by intellectual reflection. Theory was necessary to supply insights, hypotheses, logical links, explanatory interpretations and, in the end, the bases for scientific prediction. Parsons has always rejected the conception of science which sees the 'raw facts' accumulated by research as an exact transposition of reality. He rightly shows that what is called a 'fact' is already a reconstruction of reality, brought about by the conscious or unconscious resort to images, concepts and theories. The work of the theorist consists of making explicit the conceptual apparatus which the observer employs in the perception and gathering of facts, formulating it logically and widening its scope.

In Parsons's view, economics is the theoretically most advanced of all the social sciences. By concentrating on rational behaviour within a given range of activities, economics succeeded in reducing the margins of uncertainty in human conduct and has been able to work out logical models based both on induction and deduction, both on the observation of facts and on logical analysis. Parsons has great respect for economics, and is convinced that its techniques of analysis could serve as a model for sociology. In fact, Parsons's career began in economics and twenty-five years later he was to return to it. Economics left a distinct mark on his work. Parsons's interest in economics is something else which marks him out in American sociology. In general, American sociologists have shown an astonishing indifference towards economics; for the most part they are extremely ignorant of economics, whereas they frequently have a deep knowledge of psychology and especially of psycho-analysis. Coming a little later to these subjects, Parsons retained an interest in economics that is rarely found amongst American sociologists.

We have, however, only a partial view of Parsons's work if only his theoretical works are taken into account. Parsons also has a large number of empirical essays to his credit. Although calling himself an inveterate theorist, Parsons refuses to be considered only as a theorist; he has often stressed that there is an essential empirical side to all his work. But the greater part of what he calls his empirical analyses are presented in so unusual a way that, here again, Parsons is breaking with the American sociology of his time. Parsons has applied himself to three kinds of empirical research. First of all, contrary to his popular image, Parsons has done empirical research using the familiar tools of sociological enquiry; interviews, questionnaires, participant observation and quantitative data. He has in particular carried out studies of the medical profession, the aspirations of American youth, and of the academic world. Parsons is not, however, noted for this kind of empirical research, but for the other two.

In the second kind of analyses, which are better described as essays rather than research, Parsons has reflected on major problems of contemporary society. His interest in the institutions, development and crises of modern industrial society has never flagged, and has led him to explore a great variety of subjects. Thus it was no coincidence that the starting point of his work was a series of questions about capitalism. We have said that when Parsons undertook his study of Marx, Sombart, Weber, Pareto and Durkheim, he set out in the first place to compare their interpretations of the origins, history and structure of capitalist society. Later, Parsons went on to analyse almost every aspect of modern industrial society, and these essays amount to a considerable and impressive part of his work. From his empirical articles taken together it is possible to piece together an outline of the broad features of industrial societies. Parsons himself has observed that 'it is relatively rare, in the United States at least, for social scientists to attempt interpretative analyses of major aspects of the total society in which they live'.[24] Parsons is one of the rare American sociologists of the post-war period not to be afraid of going beyond the narrow confines of empirical research, in order to offer his insights to a wider public.

Parsons's third form of empirical work is perhaps more surprising. He frequently described *The Structure of Social Action* as an *empirical* study. What he observed was not some particular community or social group, but rather the ideas of certain writers. Taking these as data, he sought to pick out the major themes and to bring out what they had in common behind the superficially observable differences. By selecting authors who had worked almost completely independently of each other, Parsons set out to demonstrate even more convincingly the convergence he believed he detected in their analysis of the foundations of society, and the relationship between individual and society. The writings of Durkheim, Weber, Pareto and Marshall were the 'facts' which he attempted to report as faithfully as possible, without distorting the authors' thought and then to interpret or re-interpret them within a new framework—the general theory of action—which in his view corresponded to the underlying intention of these writers.

To his critics, Parsons could retort that his theoretical work was itself a product of the American empirical tradition, because it had what he called a 'pragmatic' quality about it. However, it is by no means certain that those who accuse him of being esoteric would be convinced by this interpretation of his work.

1.5 The Epistemological Foundations of Sociology

Another way in which Parsons differed from his colleagues in American sociology in the inter-war and post-war period was in taking an interest in epistemological problems. He did not simply take it for granted, as others have done, that sociology had a distinct and self-evident subject-matter. Clearly influenced by Max Weber, both in the way he posed the problems and the way he resolved them, he raised questions about the relationship of sociology to its subject-matter and about the validity of sociological knowledge. More precisely, Parsons raised two methodological problems : the epistemological bases of sociology as a scientific discipline, and the role of values in sociological knowledge.

If there is one thread which runs right the way through Parsons's work, it is his faith in a scientific sociology. On this, Parsons never wavered and never recanted. Sociology had to become a science and he set himself the task of making it comply with the requirements of science. This, essentially, is the vocation to which he has devoted his life and work, a vocation from which he has not strayed from his first writings to his most recent.

But it is important to understand what Parsons means by the scientific nature of sociology. First, in his view, radical empiricism is a false science or even a scientific chimera, for it is really the opposite of the true scientific spirit. At any rate, radical empiricism is not possible; the knowledge of facts implies the utilization of concepts, categories, classifications, and indeed theories. So anyone who claims to draw real scientific understanding from a direct reading of the 'facts' stands to be condemned. Parsons sees this false positivism as a betrayal both of scientific purpose and procedure.

For Parsons, science is essentially analytic, by which he means that it reconstructs reality with the aid of conceptual symbols, and these must not be confused with concrete reality. The conceptual symbols are not perfect reflections of the objective world; they are created by selecting and emphasizing certain features of reality, and these serve to structure perception and knowledge. The mental structure which symbols enable us to construct is never anything more than one particular aspect of the objective reality. So it is not necessary to demand that knowledge embodies a perfect correspondence between the objective reality and conceptual structure. For the latter is a mental construct resulting, consciously or unconsciously, from an analytical operation which puts the stress on certain selected elements at the expense of others.

This analytical procedure does not, however, result only in 'useful fictions', as Max Weber seemed to think when discussing the construction of ideal-types. Parsons defines his epistemological position as what he calls *analytical realism*.[25] By this he means that if the mental construct is not a perfect reflection of reality, it is more a reconstruction than a distortion of it. It selects aspects of reality in an effective way because there is a continuous interaction between the concept and the reality, so that by successive approximations the mental construct is continually adjusted to reality. This analytical realism constitutes the epistemological foundation on which Talcott Parsons bases his faith in scientific knowledge. Because knowledge is analytic, and because the analysis corresponds to certain aspects of objective reality, man can always aspire to knowledge less approximate than he has yet attained.

One proviso is essential: if knowledge is to be called scientific, it is valid only to the extent that it has been obtained according to the canons of scientific method. These have been rigorously worked out in the course of the last few centuries. It is becoming ever more evident that they alone can produce effective knowledge of reality—knowledge which by making possible control, prediction and manipulation, gives proof of its own validity. Parsons firmly believes that sociology must be built up through the rigorous application of these canons, and that this is the only way in which it can acquire the status of a scientific discipline. Here Parsons is equally strongly opposed to two currents of thought inherited from the nineteenth century, historicism and behaviourism, both of which he believes to have retarded the scientific progress of sociology.

The historicist school, particularly strong in Germany, considered that a social science was not possible, because human history is made up of a succession of unique and unrepeatable events, and that each civilization is a unit in itself, irreducible to anything else, and as peculiar in its structure and 'spirit' as in its history. History then became the only social science, the purpose of which was to relate and explain particulars, with no hope of ever abstracting any generalizations capable of becoming a law or general theory.

Even Max Weber, who had tried to break away from the rigid distinction first drawn by Kant between the natural sciences and the 'sciences of the spirit' (*Geisteswissenschaften*), had displayed some weakness toward historicism. Talcott Parsons followed Weber's line of thought with some amendments, and set himself the task of demonstrating the possibility and necessity of a general theory for understanding society and its history. Parsons considers this the most ambitious aspect of his work, because it involved the development of a general theory applicable to the whole field of human action. Parsons has often been attacked by the exponents of what are called middle-range theories, for which Robert Merton became the leading spokesman.[26] According to Merton, sociology is not yet ready for the construction of a general theory, but it is possible to bring it to the point of limited theories, valid for certain aspects of social reality such as, for example, a theory of small groups, a theory of organization or a theory of communication. Parsons sees this excessive timidity as a lack of confidence in scientific advance, because for him these middle-range theories have to be related to a general theory; the general theory must place them all within a single conceptual framework and link the middle-range theories to each other.

So perhaps more than any other sociologist, Parsons has stated, on the one hand, his extremely radical opposition to social historicism, and, on the other hand, the theoretical requirements which must be met if the social sciences are to become rigorously scientific. Thus for Parsons there is no break between the natural and the social sciences. The same rules of scientific method apply to both, because they rest on the same epistemological premises—those of analytic realism. This belief in the unity of scientific method is expressed in an idea which became central to Parsons's work—*the ubiquity of the concept of system*. It is only possible to conceptualize the structure of any aspect of reality mentally and theoretically if it is thought of as constituting a system in the strictest sense of the term. Briefly, for Parsons the notion of system implies the interdependence of parts, forming a whole, bound together in such a way that change and movement cannot occur in a disorderly or accidental manner, but are the outcome of a complex interaction resulting in structures and processes. Right from the start of his work, Parsons asserted the necessity of the systemic approach in scientific knowledge; sociology and the other social sciences would progress only to the extent that they developed a systemic perception of their respective subject-matters. The notion of system is absolutely central to Parsons's theoretical enterprise, and it has been the target for so many attacks that it will have to be discussed more fully later. For the moment it is enough to emphasize that for Parsons the idea of system is a major pivot of scientific analysis and consequently it is indispensable to sociology.

While asserting the scientific character of sociology, Parsons is opposed to the behaviourist view of the social sciences which, in contrast to historicism, acknowledges only objective and external knowledge of reality. To attempt to study human activity entirely from the outside, inferring nothing beyond externally observable behaviour, is to deny the existence of a whole aspect of social reality, which constitutes a mass of facts as true and real as those which can be observed from the outside. The actor's motivation, his perception, ideas, emotions and goals, his private anxieties and fears—all these are just as real, and it is essential to bring them into an explanatory model of observable behaviour.

One of Parsons's first contributions, particularly in *The Structure of Social Action*, was to emphasize that actors have motives, pursue goals, and express wishes, and that a general theory of human action must be able to integrate all these aspects of reality. Goals, wishes and motivation do not lend themselves any less to scientific analysis than do the innate or conditioned reflexes studied by Pavlov. It must be recognized that to study subjectivity in the object is not a betrayal of objectivity by the investigator. Behaviourism originated in opposition to introspectionism in psychology. This was a school of psychology which confused the subjectivity of the subject-object with the subjectivity of the subject-investigator, and believed that introspection was the only method of exploring the subjective depths of psychological existence. Since the beginning of the century, psycho-analysis has amply demonstrated the validity of an objective knowledge of subjectivity and the therapeutic use that can be made of it. In fact there has never been any contradiction between the canons of scientific method and the possibility of understanding observable reality from the inside. If the natural sciences have maintained a radical distinction between objectivity and subjectivity, it is because what they study has no subjectivity or because, as in the case of animals, it is impossible to penetrate it. For the social sciences to adopt the same radical distinction is not to imitate natural science, but rather to refuse to take account of reality as it is.

1.6 The Problem of Objectivity in Sociology

This was the conception of scientific knowledge on the basis of which Parsons raised the question of the relationship between sociology and values, long before the problem became as passionately debated as it now is in American sociology. For Parsons, whose views were again strongly influenced by Max Weber, there exist complex relationships, both of independence and interdependence, between sociology as a scientific discipline and the sociologist's own values.[27]

First of all, scientific research requires that the investigator be committed to one set of values—those of the scientific world, which can itself be seen as a sub-culture. The scientific world undeniably involves a particular ethic, to which the investigator must conform in his activities as an investigator. He must, for example, accept the pre-eminence of truth and intellectual honesty in his research. Equally, he must adhere to certain rules of scientific procedure. The internalization of this ethic is one of the essential processes in the making of a scientist. It is essential, too, in the institutionalization of science and scientific societies and associations, as well as in laboratories and research institutes. The internalization and institutionalization of the scientific ethic constitute the first and main foundation for the independence of research from other values found in society. The researcher has to accept that he must, in his professional work, give priority to the values of the scientific world over all other values in society. This can lead the scholar to abandon his country, for example, or even his research, in order to safeguard his liberty as a scientist. In short, a certain mental distance is created between that which belongs to the cultural world of science and that which belongs to the wider society. In the social sciences this distance is essential, because it is the very basis of the possibility of objectivity. Objectivity is always relative, but it is something the social scientist is always seeking, either with respect to his own society or to any other which he is studying.

Though in this respect science seeks to remain independent of the values of society, in another respect it is interdependent. The choice of problems which interest the scientist—especially the social scientist—is always conditioned both by his own values and by the values of the society of which he is part. The man of science belongs to a given historical period, to a particular civilization, and to all kinds of groups. They leave their imprint on him and continue to shape his self-conceptions as a citizen and as a human being. The scientist cannot sever all these social and cultural bonds which link him to his society and to various social groups. Nor is it either necessary or desirable that he sever them, for it is usually from his social context that he derives the values and goals on which his motivation and interest in his research is based.

Though values intervene in the selection of problems, they must not interfere with the research itself. This must be guided only by the rules of scientific method to which the investigator is committed. These help to protect him, though never completely, against his own value-judgments having too great an influence on his judgments of reality. In this way the canons of procedure help to ensure that the scientist's work is relatively value-free, while at the same time not preventing the values which originally inspired a piece of work continuing to motivate him. Parsons strongly believes that objectivity, which he sees as a kind of mental distance between the scientist and what he studies, is an essential condition for the high standing of science in modern society.

Scientific objectivity does not, however, preclude another form of interdependence between values and research, peculiar to the social sciences. Since human subjects are under investigation, knowledge of the values of the groups or individuals studied is essential. In this sense, Max Weber's *Verstehen* is in Parsons's view *a form of communication*; if he wants to understand their motivation and actions, the investigator must participate in the experience of those he is studying. But, as Parsons emphasizes, this participation must be limited : limited first in that communication can be established on the basis of particular values, without the investigator having to absorb the whole culture or participate in the wider society; limited furthermore in that the researcher's commitment to the cultural realm of science obliges him to maintain mental distance from the values of the community he is studying.

It can therefore be seen that Parsons does not deny that social values play some part in scientific research, especially in the social sciences. But, from the start, he postulates the existence of a scientific sub-culture which insulates the investigator, sets him apart and gives him a particular sense of commitment. In Parsons's view, the sociologist must restrain himself from becoming completely absorbed in the wider culture of his society. This ambivalence is the price the sociologist must pay if he aspires to the title of scientist. Whilst immersed in a civilization and its history, the sociologist also belongs to a sub-culture which imposes scientific values, modes of thought and intellectual discipline on him, and this gives him a certain distinctive reserve or reticence.

This detachment is the basis of the objectivity, even relative objectivity, which the scientist pursues; it is also the source of his respect and credibility. But this status is justified by the intellectual asceticism which he imposes on himself. For Parsons, science is a vocation in the strongest sense of the word, and throughout his life, he has sought to bear witness to this vocation.

NOTES

1. Parsons sketched his autobiography and the broad lines of his intellectual development in : 'On Building Social System Theory: A Personal History', *Daedalus*, **99** 4, 1970 pp 826–81.
2. ' "Capitalism" in Recent German Literature: Sombart and Weber', *Journal of Political Economy*, **36** 6, 1928, pp 641–61 and **37** 1, 1929, pp 31–51.

3. Parsons explained the purpose of this experiment and its consequences for teaching and research in social sciences in his article: 'Graduate Training in Social Relations at Harvard', *Journal of General Education*, **5**, 1951, pp 149–57. This innovation did not, however, spread everywhere as Parsons and his collaborators expected.
4. He gave an account of this visit to the USSR in his article 'An American's Impression of Sociology in the Soviet Union', *American Sociological Review*, **30** 1, 1965, pp 121–5.
5. 'Wants and Activities in Marshall', *Quarterly Journal of Economics*, **46** 1, 1931, pp 101–41, and 'Economics and Sociology: Marshall in Relation to the Thought of His Time', *Quarterly Journal of Economics*, **46** 2, 1932, pp 316–47.
6. L. J. Henderson, *Pareto's General Sociology: A Physiologist's Interpretation* (Cambridge, Harvard University Press, 1935). See also Bernard Barber (ed), *L. J. Henderson on the Social System* (Chicago, Chicago University Press, 1970).
7. Talcott Parsons, 'Pareto', in *Encylopaedia of the Social Sciences*, 1933, vol 2, pp 576–8; 'Pareto's Central Analytical Scheme', *Journal of Social Philosophy*, **1** 3, 1936, pp 244–62.
8. 'On Building Social System Theory: A Personal History', *op cit*, pp 828–9.
9. See in particular Talcott Parsons, 'Durkheim's Contribution to the Theory of Integration of Social Systems', in his *Sociological Theory and Modern Society* (1967) chapter 1.
10. The term 'positivism' has acquired quite a variety of meanings, and that at which Parsons tilts has precious little in common with the positivism of Comte, who strongly emphasized the role of 'subjectivity' [see Marvin Harris, *The Rise of Anthropological Theory* (New York, Thomas Y. Crowell Co., 1968) chapter 18, and especially the discussion of Comte in Norbert Elias, *Was ist Soziologie?* (München, Juventa Verlag, 1970) (chapter 1)]. When he speaks of positivism, Parsons usually has in mind crude empiricism or even behaviourism. (SJM)
11. On the Chicago School and the parts Robert Park and Ernest W. Burgess played in it, see particularly R. E. L. Faris, *Chicago Sociology, 1920–32* (San Francisco, Chandler Publishing Company, 1967).
12. R. E. Park, *Race and Culture* (Glencoe, Ill., Free Press, 1950); W. I. Thomas and F. Znaniecki, *The Polish Peasant in Europe and America* vols 1 and 2 (Chicago, Chicago University Press, 1918), vols 3–5 (Boston, Richard D. Badger, 1920); Louis Wirth, *The Ghetto* (Chicago, University of Chicago Press, 1928); E. Franklin Frazier, *The Negro Family in the United States* (Chicago, University of Chicago Press, 1939); Everett C. and Helen M. Hughes: *Where Peoples Meet: Racial and Ethnic Frontiers* (Glencoe, Ill., Free Press, 1952).
13. E. H. Sutherland, *The Professional Thief* (Chicago, University of Chicago Press, 1937) and *White Collar Crime* (New York, Dryden, 1949); F. M. Thrasher, *The Gang* (Chicago, University of Chicago Press, 2nd ed, 1936); R. E. L. Faris and H. W. Dunham, *Mental Disorders in Urban Areas* (Chicago, University of Chicago Press, 1939); C. R. Shaw and H. D. McKay, *Social Factors in Juvenile Delinquency* (Washington, US Printing Office, 1939) and *Juvenile Delinquency and Urban Areas* (Chicago, University of Chicago Press, 1942).
14. The five volumes, generally known as the Yankee City Series, were

summarized by Warner himself under the title *Yankee City* (New York, Yale University Press, 1963).

15. Robert S. Lynd and Helen M. Lynd, *Middletown: A Study in American Culture* (New York, Harcourt, Brace and World, 1929), followed by *Middletown in Transition: A Study in Cultural Conflicts* (New York, Harcourt, Brace and World, 1937).

16. A. Davis, Burleigh and Mary Gardner, *Deep South* (Chicago, University of Chicago Press, 1941).

17. James West, *Plainville, USA* (New York, Columbia University Press, 1945).

18. William Foote Whyte, *Street Corner Society* (Chicago, University of Chicago Press, 1943).

19. Talcott Parsons, 'Cooley and the Problem of Internalization', in *Cooley and Sociological Analysis* edited by A. J. Reiss Jr (Ann Arbor, University of Michigan Press, 1968) p 48.

20. W. I. Thomas, *On Social Organization and Social Personality: Selected Papers*, edited with an Introduction by Morris Janowitz (Chicago, University of Chicago Press, 1970); C. H. Cooley, *Human Nature and the Social Order* (New York, Charles Scribner's Sons, 1902); G. H. Mead, *Mind, Self and Society* (Chicago, University of Chicago Press, 1934).

21. The two most important volumes of Simmel's work to have appeared in English are *The Sociology of George Simmel*, edited and translated by Kurt H. Wolff (Glencoe, Ill., Free Press, 1950) and *'Conflict' and 'The Web of Group Affiliations'*, translated by K. H. Wolff and R. Bendix (Glencoe, Ill., Free Press, 1955). A list of Simmel's works which had been translated into English prior to 1950 is given in the Introduction to the former book, together with a bibliography of American studies on Simmel.

22. Guy Perrin has said that 'it is difficult to conceive of a clearer or more precise presentation of the essential machinery of the Paretian mechanism' than that given by Parsons. [*Sociologie de Pareto* (Paris, Presses Universitaires de France, 1966) p 4.]

23. The omission is the more striking because these and other American writers had anticipated several aspects of the 'voluntaristic theory of action'. See Roscoe C. Hinkle, 'Antecedents of the Action Orientation in American Sociology before 1935', *American Sociological Review*, **28** 5, 1963, pp 705–15. (SJM)

24. Talcott Parsons, 'The Distribution of Power in American Society', in his *Politics and Social Structure* (1969) p 185.

25. See in particular on this *The Structure of Social Action* (1937), chapter 19, especially pp 728–31.

26. R. K. Merton, *Social Theory and Social Structure*, enlarged ed (New York, Free Press, 1968), chapter 2. (SJM)

27. Parsons explains his position on this question particularly in his article 'Evaluation and Objectivity in Social Science: An Interpretation of Max Weber's Contributions', in his *Sociological Theory and Modern Society* (1967), chapter 3.

2. The General Theory of Action

Talcott Parsons has progressively developed a conception of the content of sociology and of its place among the social sciences that is quite his own. Very few sociologists have taken so much trouble in drawing the boundaries of sociology, tracing its outlines, describing its connections with related disciplines and sketching a complete map of the social sciences. Parsons could be said to have produced a sort of 'ecology' of sociology, since he has sought to place it within the 'environment' of the other sciences of man, and to analyse the connections between them all. As a result, Parsons's work goes far beyond sociology alone because it is ultimately concerned with the whole of the social sciences. Parsons has always described himself as a sociologist, but it is clear that his work cannot be approached only as sociology.

So the widest possible view of Parsons's work has to be taken, if what are perhaps its more original and certainly its most daring aspects are not to be missed. For this reason, this chapter begins by following Parsons onto the highest level of analysis, that of *the general theory of action*. In later chapters, we shall then be better able to understand Parsons's sociological theory within the general perspective.[1]

2.1 The Idea of Social Action

The starting point of the whole Parsonian theory is the idea of social action, which he elaborates into a vast framework. It is an idea which allows of no precise and strict definition, often to the despair of Parsons's readers. However, Parsons has explained repeatedly and quite explicitly what he means by it. Social action, in the sense in which he uses it, is all human behaviour motivated and directed by the meanings which the actor discerns in the external world, meanings of which he takes account and to which he responds. So the essential feature of social action is the actor's sensitivity to the meanings of the people and things about him, his perception of these meanings and his reactions to the messages they convey.

Since it is primarily defined by its meaningfulness, social action must be interpreted from the actor's subjective point of view. That includes his perception not only of his environment, but of the feelings, ideas and motives which shape his own actions, and of others' reactions to his actions. It must be emphasized that the actor in question can be an individual but it may also be a group, an organization, a region, a total society, or a civilization. *Parsons avoids conflating social action with individual behaviour.* On the contrary, he generalizes the idea to any entity, individual or collective, of which the behaviour can be analysed in terms of the meanings it implies.

Moreover, the notion of social action does not confine the observer only to the actor's subjective point of view. On the contrary, taking note of this subjectivity leads on to the analysis of social action in terms of the duality of action and situation, which is fundamental to the whole Parsonian theory of action. Parsons's actor is a being-in-a-situation, for his action is always the outcome of his reading of a complex of signs which he perceives in his environment and to which he responds. The individual actor's environment is not only the physical surroundings in which he acts —the material objects, climatic conditions, the geography and geology of the area, but also his own biological organism. The actor feels the influence and import of these objects, accounts for them, develops feelings about them, and uses them for ends which he imposes on them. All these relations with the physical environment suppose a set of interpretations through which the actor perceives reality and which gives his actions a sense of direction.

But the most important objects in the actor's environment are clearly social objects—in the first place, other actors. With these, social action becomes interaction. Analysis of the actor's subjectivity now becomes double or multi-faceted : to the subjectivity of ego there is a corresponding subjectivity of alter, who in turn may be individual or collective. In all his work, Parsons shows the complexity of social relationships between people. The interaction between two or more actors and the subjectivity involved in it is one of the main pivots of Parsonian theory.

Another category of social objects which Parsons regards as very important are cultural or symbolic objects. Because it is essentially meaningful, social action necessarily involves symbolism. It is through signs and symbols that the actor discerns, experiences, evaluates and manipulates his environment. Symbolism is essential in social interaction to communication in all its forms. By communication actors are linked together. Action and interaction therefore take place within a vast symbolic universe, from which each action acquires a meaning both for the actor and for others.

Another function of symbolism in social action is in making possible the rules of conduct, norms and values which guide the actor in the orientation of his action. Norms and values indeed are essentially symbolic in nature. In the first place, they make actors' conduct communicable : human action, because of the norms and values to which it relates, becomes less opaque to other actors, as well as to the performing actor, because they can all read a meaning, orientation and continuity into it. Second, it is through norms and values that the actor is able to interpret a situation, to discern within it the landmarks, limits and forces of which he must take account in his behaviour. Third, norms and values supply the actor with goals and means which serve as a guide to him and at the same time give his actions a particular meaning both for himself and for others.

Human action, as Parsons emphasizes, is bounded by two spheres of 'non-action' forming two distinct kinds of constraint. The first is the physical environment, which includes such aspects of reality as climate, natural resources, available tools and techniques, the biological constitution of individuals, the givens of heredity and temperament. This first class of constraints is common to all living things and comprises a complex of conditions with which all action has to reckon. The second sphere of constraints is that of the symbolic or cultural environment which designates goals to be attained and the appropriate means, establishes the permissible limits of action, defines priorities and suggests choices. The cultural sphere makes human action unique among all the possible forms of action. It is because it assumes a normative and symbolic character that human action differs from every other kind of action.

It follows from what has been said that social action, with which all Parsons's work is concerned, comprises four elements :

1. *a subject-actor*, which can be an individual, a group or a collectivity;

2. *a situation*, comprising the physical and social objects to which the actor relates;

3. *symbols*, by means of which the actor relates to the different elements of the situation and attributes meaning to them;

4. *rules, norms and values*, which guide the orientation of action—the actor's relations with the social and non-social objects in his environment.

2.2 Systems of Social Action

In Parsons's view, all the social sciences study social action in the sense just described. Another problem must now be tackled. For the study of social action to become truly scientific in the most rigorous sense it is necessary, according to Parsons, to postulate that *human action always exhibits the properties of a system*. We have already said that for Parsons the notion of system is essential to science. Parsons became quite convinced of this through the work of Vilfredo Pareto and his American disciple and interpreter L. J. Henderson. From his first writings and throughout his work, Parsons has investigated the systemic elements in human action of every kind. If there is one thing of which Parsons is certain, it is that the social sciences can only be scientific to the extent that they resort to systemic analysis, as did the physical sciences and, more recently, biology.

Human action does in fact lend itself very well to systemic analysis. All action can be seen as a complex of unit-acts involving one or more actors; it can be broken down into gestures, words and performances. Put together again as a whole, these form for example a social role (the role of father of a family or head of an office) or an episode of interaction between two or more people. These techniques of analysis and synthesis have been used empirically in a good number of small-group studies. Thus Robert Bales worked out categories which permit every intervention by participants in a group discussion to be broken down into small units, classified, and then rearranged or synthesized to reveal facts about

the interaction which were not at first apparent.[2] Action, on whatever level of reality, is always a compound, a product of synthesis
which can be analytically broken down. At the same time, no action
can ever be considered in isolation. It is always linked with other
actions and with them forms a larger whole. Thus the role of the
father in a family is one element in a complex of actions which
constitutes the family. And this in its turn forms part of the larger
framework of kinship, and so on. In consequence, any action can be
considered both as a complex of unit-acts and as an element within
a still larger whole.

This interdependence among units of action gives support to the
idea of the system of action, insofar as any system involves the
interrelation of parts constituting a whole. But this is not sufficient
to justify what has been said about systems of action. Parsons's
conception of a system is something much more complex. For him,
a system must fulfil three conditions. The first is a *structural* condition : the units of a system and the system itself must meet
certain organizational requirements, constituting relatively stable
features or components which can serve as points of reference for
systemic analysis. According to Parsons, normative patterns and,
at the highest level of abstraction, the 'pattern variables' perform
this role in systems of action. The second condition implies the
notion of *function* : if a system of action is to exist and maintain
itself in existence, certain elementary needs of the system, as a
system, must be met. This is the problem of functional prerequisites,
or of the functional dimensions of systems of action. The third condition refers to the system's internal dynamics : by its very nature
a system implies variations and changes which occur not by chance
but according to certain principles and rules.

The general theory of action consists principally of the analysis
of these three aspects of systems of action. We shall now look in a
little more detail at Parsons's thinking on each of them.

One thing must be mentioned first. For Parsons, a system of
action is not something concrete, like a family or factory. As he
uses it, the system of action is a mode of conceptualization and
analysis; it is a means of mentally reconstructing reality, a way of
conceiving things—in short a heuristic procedure. There is nothing
in reality of which we can say 'this is a system of action'. However
any action on any level of reality—whether it be the behaviour of

two people towards each other, class conflict or international hostilities—can be analysed as a system. The idea of a system of action is one of great generality, and does not correspond directly with anything in reality, because it is an analytical tool with an extremely wide range of applications.

2.3 Cultural Patterns—The Structural Elements of Systems of Action

To return to the basic elements of any system of action, two components are essential—an actor and his situation, the latter made up of physical and social objects. At its simplest, *a system of action means the organization of interactional relations between the actor and his situation.* Actually, interaction as such does not always occur. True interaction involves other actors ('social objects' in Parsons's language) in complementary action and reciprocal influence. In the case of physical objects, the actor either has to act upon them, adapting them to his purpose, or has to adapt himself to them. As for symbolic or cultural objects, the actor uses these to communicate with other actors, or refers to them as guides for the orientation of his action towards physical objects and other actors. But these distinctions do not change the nature of social action as Parsons conceives of it.

Having reduced the system of action to its basic elements, the first question to consider is how relations between the actor and objects in his environment can exist and endure. In other words, what factors structure action and interaction so that they persist in relative stability?

What disconcerts many of Parsons's critics is his permanent fascination with *order*. Through the influence of Marxist and socialist theorists, conflict and change have come to be emphasized in the analysis of action. Investigating the social foundations of order, Parsons could not avoid acquiring a reputation as a social conservative interested only in maintaining the *status quo*. His critics have, however, too readily transposed what is essentially an analytical problem onto the ideological plane. They forget that for Parsons, *social order is less a fact than a problem.* Certainly, after even the most superficial observation, it has to be recognized that human action—whether individual or collective—is not random.

It is neither chaotic nor unpredictable. There is no longer a war of all against all. Some kind of order is observable in individual as well as collective action, so that the actor is able accurately to predict his own behaviour and that of others around him. But this order, which can be discerned in so many forms, persists as a problem to be constantly resolved. The question always remains : what is the basis of order in social action? What is surprising is not that there are conflicts and struggles, but that there is a certain order which persists below all the causes of disorganization in individual and collective action.

In taking up the problem of order Parsons was following in the footsteps of the great philosophers who examined the nature of human society. He put himself directly in the tradition of Hobbes, Locke, Rousseau and Mill. Like them, he considered that order could not be taken for granted, but had to be explained. But their explanations had not been satisfactory. Order could not be considered the result of an accidental and spontaneous convergence of diverse interests, as Locke believed. It is not the product of a social contract, as Rousseau would have it. Nor, *pace* Hobbes, is it the outcome of all men submitting to one authority in order to avoid permanent conflict. All these interpretations have a fundamental defect : they are based on the assumptions that human action is motivated by self-interest, and that order comes about in the teeth of individualism and disparate interests. This simplistic psychology of classical utilitarianism was greatly undermined by the more recent work of the principal precursors of modern social science, who opened the way to a new and genuinely scientific interpretation of order. And this reinterpretation of order in social action constitutes, for Parsons, the greatest achievement of the social sciences in the first half of the twentieth century.

Parsons has often emphasized surprising convergences in the work of various theorists, but most of all between Freud and Durkheim. Starting from very different positions, these two writers— though unaware of each other's work—converged to such an extent that their writings are complementary. Both showed that human action follows *rules, norms* and *patterns* which structure it and give it a coherent framework. In Freud's work, rules of conduct appear in the form of the super-ego, which is made up of sanctions and significant symbols forming the personality's moral conscience. In Durkheim, rules and patterns are called *représentations collectives* and *conscience collective*; when an individual's action is performed subject to their constraint, Durkheim calls it a 'social fact'.

There is one important difference between Freud's and Durkheim's points of view, which at the same time makes their contribution complementary. Freud locates cultural patterns in the structure of the individual personality, whereas Durkheim locates *représentations collectives* in society. For Freud, cultural patterns exist to the extent that they are *internalized* by the person and form an integral part of the psychological organization of the personality. For Durkheim patterns exist in so far as they are *institutionalized,* so that they can exercise an external constraint over people's moral consciences.

These two perspectives are far from contradictory. Parsons has tried to show that they are really complementary and are two sides of the same coin. More precisely, the two perspectives require each other, each finding support in the other. The external patterns which are internalized by the personality to become the super-ego are the same as those which are institutionalized, to the extent that they are shared by a plurality of people. Conversely, the patterns are institutionalized because a plurality of people have internalized them. So Freud's moral conscience merges with Durkheim's *conscience collective*; the super-ego is the individualized counterpart of the *représentations collectives* which exist in society.

In this complementarity of the individual and the collective perspectives, Parsons sees the solution to the problem of order posed by Hobbes, Locke, Rousseau and Mill. The basis of order is in the structure of systems of action, in the patterns, norms and values which have meaning for the individual actor or collectivity, in the fact that they are internalized in the personality and at the same time institutionalized in society and culture. Parsons himself sums up his thinking as follows

> The most fundamental theorem of the theory of action seems to me to be that the *structure* of systems of action *consists* in institutionalized (in social and cultural systems) and/or internalized (in personalities and organisms) patterns of cultural meaning. That this is not a proposition obvious to common sense is attested

by the long and complex history of behaviouristic and other reductionist theories of human behaviour . . .[3]

This theorem is really central to Parsons's work, for it explains the complementarity of the individual and collective perspectives by showing that it rests on the dual character of cultural patterns, which exist both in people's minds and in the symbolic universe of society. So, returning to the elements of systems of action, the same patterns can be found in the actor and in the situation, because they have been internalized by other actors and institutionalized into culture and social structures.

2.4 The Pattern Variables of Systems of Action

As we have just seen, cultural patterns serve to structure systems of action. But Parsons, pushing his analysis still further, shows that they themselves are structured in a particular way. By their very nature cultural patterns force the actor to make choices and judgments which compel him to take sides—to choose some thing or some form of behaviour instead of another. Action guided by values is therefore necessarily both a choice of one thing and a refusal of another, a move in one direction and a retreat in another, a yes and a no. In short, duality and contradiction are inherent in the realm of values.

Other sociologists before Parsons had already spotlighted this duality. This was particularly so with Ferdinand Tönnies, who developed the theory of two basic categories of social organization, *Gemeinschaft* (community) and *Gesellschaft* (society), or rather *gemeinschaftlich* and *gesellschaftlich* relationships. Each of these two types of social relationship was a distillation of a set of patterns and values defining human nature and social life. Tönnies himself had a clear preference for the *gemeinschaftlich* forms of social life, in which he saw a superior morality. Parsons returned to Tönnies's dichotomy, which he considered to be the first and incomplete statement of a structural distinction in the analysis of action. Parsons's principal objection to the dichotomy was that it was too sweeping a generalization, concealing several different dimensions which needed to be made explicit.[4] This became apparent to Parsons in the course of his first piece of empirical research, an analysis of the social role of the doctor. He was able to show that in certain respects medical practice called for *gemeinschaftlich* relationships and in other respects for *gesellschaftlich*. Thus, doctor and patient form a community of interest, in that their common objective, which dominates their whole relationship, is the health or recovery of the patient. But at the same time, the doctor–patient relationship must in certain respects be *gesellschaftlich* in charactor; the patient must accept a specific rather than a diffuse relationship with the doctor—merely as a patient, not as a friend.

So Tönnies's antithesis between *Gemeinschaft* and *Gesellschaft* is not uni-dimensional, as he believed, but multi-dimensional. It is important to disentangle the various dimensions involved. Parsons sees these dimensions as a serious of dilemmas confronting every social actor, who has to resolve them in the orientation of his action. There is not, as Tönnies thought, one dilemma but several. They are not, however, unlimited in number, for in every society and every social relationship, there are only a few basic and elementary options. Parsons hesitated as to whether there existed four, five or six dilemmas,[5] and finally asserted that he could distinguish four. These four dilemmas, each offering two possible responses, Parsons calls the *pattern variables*.

As we have mentioned, Parsons began to develop the idea of pattern variables in the course of his analysis of professional roles. The first outlines can be seen in his attempt to find a better way of distinguishing between the liberal professions and the business world than that in common use; instead of speaking of the 'disinterestedness' of the former and the pursuit of self-interest by the latter, Parsons looked for variables which were less utilitarian and more sociological.[6] Then, in *The Social System*,[7] he used the same variables in a revised form in his analysis of the medical profession itself; here the pattern variables were exclusively sociological concepts. But in *Toward a General Theory of Action* it became apparent that the pattern variables could be applied much more widely and that they belonged at the most general level of analysis—the general theory of action.

During the years between *The Structure of Social Action* (1937) and *Working Papers in the Theory of Action* (1953), the pattern variables were the main pivot of Parsons's general theory of action. Later, he introduced new elements which we shall discuss further on, but the pattern variables continue to play a central role in Parsonian theory. Here is how Parsons himself explains the four variables in his most recent writings.

First the actor may judge a physical or social object according to criteria applicable to a whole range of objects, thereby opting for *universalism*. On the other hand, he can look at the ways in which the object is unique, judging it in itself, according to criteria peculiar to this object and its context, thereby opting for *particularism*. For example, a teacher judges and evaluates his pupils according to certain general criteria which give his judgments a just and equitable basis. In contrast, a father judges his child according to criteria more particular to his child than if he were his teacher. That does not prevent a degree of particularism entering into the teacher's judgment, nor the father to a certain extent making universalistic assessments of his children. But the dominant note is *universalism* in the teacher's case and *particularism* in the father's. It is this disparate emphasis which Parsons sees as the different response to a dilemma.

Second, the actor can judge a physical or social object according to what it does, achieves or effects; his judgment is based on the object's *performance*. On the other hand the actor may attribute importance to the object in itself, independently of its achievement or its benefit to the actor. In this case, judgment is based on a *quality* of the object.[8]

Third, the actor must choose between *affective neutrality* and *affectivity* in his relationships with objects in his situation. He chooses affective neutrality when he sets his own feelings or emotions aside, for the benefit of an instrumental relationship orientated to ends external to the relationship itself. As a general rule, relationships in the occupational sphere are dominated by affective neutrality. It is only in certain contexts, such as the family or friendship that affectivity can be more freely expressed in social relationships.

Fourth, the actor may be in contact with other actors only in certain specific ways and not totally involved with them. In other words, the actor may have a relationship with many people as clients, patients or employees. This is the option of *specificity*. The option of *diffuseness* on the other hand means that he is involved in more total relationships, related to other actors by multiple ties, involved as a whole person. Again, the teacher's relationship with his pupils is rather specific, whilst that of the father with his children is more diffuse.

It can be seen at once that these four pattern variables are an amplification of Tönnies's dichotomy. Universalism, performance, affective neutrality and specificity comprise Tönnies's *gesellschaftlich* relationships; particularism, quality, affectivity and diffuseness are the typical patterns in *gemeinschaftlich* relationships. The advantage of these distinctions over Tönnies's dichotomy is that they are clearly more flexible. They permit the analysis of relationships in which, for example, universalism and performance, or affectivity and specificity are intermingled. In other words, Parsons's variables served to extend the usefulness of Tönnies's dichotomy by disentangling dimensions which Tönnies had conflated.

Since *Toward a General Theory of Action* (1951) Parsons has maintained that the pattern variables are the essential components of any system of action. This means that he sees the variables as having very great analytical generality. They can be applied to individual or collective behaviour, to the analysis of small groups or whole societies, to describing the actions of individual actors or social institutions.

However, Parsons thought he could divide the four variables into two classes, for they do not all relate to the same elements in the system of action. Two of the variables pertain particularly to the object to which the actor relates, to the meaning the object has for the actor and the kind of judgment which is called for from the actor. These variables are universalism/particularism and quality/performance. Parsons calls these the *pattern variables of the modality of the object.*[9]

The second pair of variables, diffuseness/specificity and affectivity/affective neutrality, pertain to the actor and define his attitude towards the object and the type of relationship which he has with it. Parsons therefore calls these *pattern variables of orientation to the object.*

Thus we return to the actor–situation duality which is central to the system of action. The variables of object modality relate to the situation and the objects within it; the variables of orientation to the object relate to the actor. So the role of the four pattern variables in structuring systems of action is made very clear.

2.5 The Functional Prerequisites of Systems of Action

If analysing the structure of action points to the factors contributing to the stability of the system, the functional dimensions of systems of action draw attention to processes within it. Parsons defines the function of any living system as *a complex of activities directed towards meeting a need or needs of the system qua system.* The idea of function as Parsons understands it is therefore essential to systemic analysis, or at least for the analysis of systems of action. As Parsons puts it :

> the concept function is central to the understanding of all living systems. Indeed, it is simply the corollary of the concept living system, delineating certain features in the first instance of the system–environment relation and in the second, of the internal differentiation of the system itself.[10]

This quotation reveals the double mode of analysing systems of action which Parsons always uses. First, any complex of behaviour which can be treated as a system of action (for example, a professional role or a social class) also forms part of a wider whole, to which it is related in many ways. For it is both dependent on the wider whole and at the same time to some extent contributes to the whole. A first group of system needs springs from this— those which relate to the system's relations with its environment. Second, the system of action is itself composed of parts or units which are related to each other both by differentiation and integration. A second group of system needs pertaining to the exigencies of its internal organization appear here.

If a system is functioning and maintaining itself, it must be responding to these two kinds of needs or problems. This implies that it is able to organize and mobilize the necessary activities. That is the Parsonian conception of function. So inside a system of action are to be found functions or complexes of activities, some dealing with the system's relations with its environment and others with its internal organizational needs.

Parsons suggests a second way of looking at the functions of a system of action, this time springing from his distinction between the system's goals and the means at its disposal for attaining them. Parsons calls 'consummatory' those activities of the system directed towards the attainment of desired ends (be they goods, gratifications or ideals) and 'instrumental' those which involve the acquisition and utilization of means.

These two ways of looking at the problem of needs and functions of systems, in terms of the external/internal and ends/means distinctions, can be superimposed on each other. Thus there are goals implying relations with the environment and others which concern the internal organization of the system, and so on. In consequence, the simultaneous use of these two distinctions reveals that *in any system of action four functions must be present* if the four elementary system needs identified by Parsons are to be satisfied. Indeed, a system of action only exists if these four needs are at least partially fulfilled, and if the four functions exist to some extent. This is why Parsons claims that *the four functions are functional prerequisites of any system of action.*

Parsons also represented the basic functions as four 'dimensions' of the system of action, in the precise sense in which the term is used in physics. In other words, at any moment in the life of a system of action, the unit-acts which comprise it must all be located in one or other of the four dimensions. And if a unit-act could be plotted during the whole time in which the system of action persists—which is possible in physics—it would be observed to move like a particle from one dimension to another, as the system of action gradually changed. At the same time the movement of each unit-act is itself a factor in modifying the system.

The four functions or dimensions of a system of action are as follows. First, what Parsons calls *adaptation* is the complex of unit-acts which serve to establish relations between the system and its external environment. As Parsons defines it, the external environment of a system of action is generally another system or several systems, whether action or non-action systems. Adaptation consists of taking diverse resources needed by the system from the environing systems, in exchange for products originating within the system itself, and arranging and transforming these resources to serve the needs of the system. As its name implies, this function includes activities by which the system adapts to its environment and the constraints, exigencies and limits it imposes, as well as those activities by which the system adapts the environment to its needs, modifying, controlling and exploiting it.

Goal-attainment is the second dimension of any system of action. Parsons puts in this category all actions which serve to define the goals of the system, to mobilize and manage resources and effort to attain goals and gratification. It is just this capacity for establishing goals and methodically pursuing them which distinguishes systems of action from non-action systems—i.e. physical or biological systems.

There are certain unit-acts in every system of action, the purpose of which is to establish control, to inhibit deviant tendencies, to maintain co-ordination between parts, and to avoid too serious disturbances. Parsons names this complex of actions *integration*. This is the stabilizing dimension of the system comprising actions which tend to protect the system against sudden changes and major disturbances, maintaining the coherence or 'solidarity' necessary to its survival and functioning.

Lastly, any system of action needs a complex of unit-acts which supply actors with necessary motivation. In a way, this means that every system of action has to accumulate a reservoir of motivation, which, because it is always being drawn upon, needs to be continually replenished. The system always needs at least a minimal level of motivational energy. So this function is like a sort of system of mains, which accumulates and distributes energy in the form of motivation. That is why Parsons gave this dimension the name of *latency or pattern maintenance*.[11] The pattern-maintenance function is the point of contact between systems of action and the symbolic and cultural universe. The latter has a special bearing on systems of action in that it supplies them with symbols, ideas, modes of expression and judgments necessary for the creation of motivation and its direction towards action.

Using the internal/external and instrumental/consummatory distinctions in a cross-break yields a classification of the four functions arranged as in Fig. 1.[12] Since *Working Papers in the Theory of Action* (1953) in which Parsons set it out for the first time, the four-function paradigm has become central to all his work, in which it continually recurs in many different forms. As the table is normally read clockwise, Parsons refers to the four functions by the abbreviation AGIL.

At this point, Parsons's work must be linked with the name of Robert Bales, for it was to him that Parsons owed the formulation

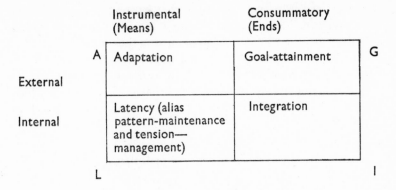

Fig. 1 The Functional Paradigm of Systems of Action

of the four functions. After *Toward a General Theory of Action* (1951) in which he had much extended the scope of the pattern variables, applying the idea to the general theory of action, Parsons was looking for a way to relate the total functioning of systems of action to the four pattern variables. It was then that he was struck by the convergence between his research and the work of his Harvard colleague, Robert Bales. Bales was then working on the analysis of interaction between members of small experimental groups formed to solve prescribed problems. This led him to formulate categories for classifying each participant's every action. Bales had grouped the categories he used under four headings, corresponding to what he had called the 'functional problems' of the group. Parsons finally adopted Bales's formulation of the functional problems, though modifying it slightly. In passing, it is worth noting that it was through Bales that Parsons came to draw on the long tradition of American research on the social psychology of small groups. He thus became reconciled with American sociology, drawing ideas from it which became central to his theory.

In order to incorporate Bales's ideas into his general theory, and to generalize categories derived from the micro-sociological level to all systems of action, Parsons had to accept the postulate of the unity of micro-sociology and macro-sociology. But as he had already long accepted the still more general unity of all systems of action from biological to sociological, it was not difficult for him to recognize the unity of micro- and macro-sociology.

It must not be thought, however, that Parsons's borrowings from Bales prevented him from continuing to work with the pattern variables. On the contrary, he proceeded to show the links between the pattern variables and functional dimensions. The connection is logical. Activities in response to a particular functional exigency, such as adaptation, require types of behaviour from actors which are different from activities in response to other functions such as

Universalism (O)   Affectivity (S)
(Neutrality) (M)   (Particularism) (M)

	A		G	
Specificity (O) (Performance) (M)	Adaptation	Goal-attainment	Performance (O) (Specificity) (M)
Quality (O) (Diffuseness) (M)	Pattern-maintenance	Integration	Diffuseness (O) (Quality) (M)
	L		I	

Neutrality (O)   Particularism (O)
(Universalism) (M)   (Affectivity) (M)

O = Pattern Variable of attitude or orientation to the object
M = Pattern Variable of object-modality

Fig. 2 Relations between the Pattern Variables and the Functional Dimensions of Systems of Action

goal-attainment. In adaptive activities, the actor/situation relationship is geared to different objectives and consequently governed by different rules from those which apply to goal-attainment. It may therefore be expected that each of the four functions corresponds to a particular set of pattern variables, relating both to object-modality and orientation to the object.

It is not possible here to tell the full story of how Parsons came to arrange the pattern variables in relation to each of the four functions.[13] Figure 2 sums it all up. It should be noted that each of the four functions is associated with two pattern variable options of object-modality and two of orientation to the object.[14]

2.6 The Sub-systems of Action

The four-function schema allowed Parsons to refine his thinking on another point. Probably influenced by Sorokin,[15] Parsons had long insisted that social action necessarily implied the intersection of three systems : personality, culture and social systems. The contribution each makes to action can be distinguished analytically, although any concrete action as a whole involves all three systems at once. Parsons added in passing that a fourth system, the biological organism, was also involved.

Analysing the functional dimensions of action led Parsons to introduce the organism into his scheme and to give it more prominence than perhaps any other sociologist. The division of the system of action into four distinct functions allowed the elaboration of a theoretical model of the relationships between the organism, personality, culture and social system. This model is essential to understanding the whole of Parsons's work.

It became apparent to Parsons that at the highest level of analysis, the biological organism, personality, culture and social system could be thought of as the four most general sub-systems of systems of action. He came to the conclusion that these four sub-systems were related to each other in the same way as the four functions of a system of action. *The biological organism corresponds to the function of adaptation,* in the sense that it mediates relations

A   G

Biological organism (Adaptation)	Personality (Goal-attainment)
Culture (Pattern-maintenance)	Social system (Integration)

L   I

Fig. 3 The Sub-systems of the General System of Action

with the physical world, adapting to it, manipulating it or transforming it. It is through the organism that the system both adapts
to the environment and adapts the environment to its needs. *The
personality corresponds to the function of goal-attainment*. It is
within and through the personality system that objectives are defined and resources and energy mobilized for the attainment of the
desired goals. *The social system represents the function of integration*. It is this which creates solidarity, generates loyalties, defines
the limits of permissible action and imposes constraints. *Culture
represents the function of latency or pattern-maintenance*. It supplies actors with motivation and support for their actions, by means
of the norms, ideals, values and ideologies which it makes available
or even imposes on them.

Parsons insists, however, that these four sub-systems do not all
contribute to the general system of action in the same way or to
the same extent. Of the biological organism, only that part of its
activities which contributes to the meaningful behaviour is relevant
to the system of action. Thus, those of the organism's movements
which are unconscious and unwilled, like the beating of the heart
and circulation of blood, do not belong to the system of action. As
for the personality and social system, they are the real field of action
and fall entirely within the system of action. Culture is the least
'active' of the sub-systems, because, in itself, it does not act. It gives
the actor motivation and guides his action, but it remains outside
action as such. The cultural sub-system contributes to action without becoming totally involved in it like the personality, social system
and biological organism.

The inter-relations between the four sub-systems are very complex. Each can, in a way, be considered as an independent system.
It is analytically possible to look at each one and its particular
characteristics and activities in isolation. What Parsons calls the
'boundaries' of each of the sub-systems can be marked out; these
demarcation lines distinguish each sub-system from the others. But
though independent, the four sub-systems are also interdependent.
They rely upon each other, support and complement each other.
The personality cannot exist without the organism, nor without
the nexus of interrelations with the social system and the symbolic
universe of culture. Similarly, to the social system the personality's
motivation is absolutely essential, as is culture's symbolic and

normative contribution. And culture only exists because it is realized in personality and in the social system's network of interaction.
So none of the four sub-systems is reducible to any of the others, but
each is necessarily and strictly related to the rest. This is what
Parsons means when he says that these are 'boundary maintaining
systems', but that they are also 'open boundary systems'.

Across these open boundaries between the sub-systems, there are
continual interchanges. There is a constant coming and going of
'products', circulating from one sub-system to another. What Parsons means by this, and the central place the analysis of these
interrelations occupies in his theoretical model, is discussed in more
detail in later chapters.

One last aspect of this scheme must, however, be emphasized
now. Each of these relatively independent sub-systems can be
treated as a system and can in turn be broken down into four sub-
systems, again following the model of the four basic functions. These
new sub-systems can also in their turn be taken as systems and
analysed in the same way. Parsons's system of action is like a set
of Chinese boxes—when one is opened, it contains a smaller one,
which contains a smaller one still, and so on. This means that for
analytical purposes, any sub-system on any level can be taken as,
in Parsons's terminology, the *system of reference*. This approach
gives the Parsonian model very great flexibility, and at the same
time scarcely less great a complexity. It is particularly important
when using Parsons's model not to lose sight of the system of reference initially adopted, and not to confuse levels of analysis. These
rules are not always followed, and the resulting errors of interpretation are often attributed to the Parsonian model when they
really arise from the use made of it.

2.7 The Dynamics of Systems of Action

After structure and functions, the third requirement of a system
of action, if it is to be a system, is some organization in its internal
dynamics. In a system, the central purpose of which is precisely
action and activity, this third condition is obviously essential.

By its very nature, action involves change, the disturbance of an
existing state and transition to a new and sometimes novel state.
By his action, an actor intervenes in a situation, and this almost

inevitably entails at least a minor transformation either of the situation or the actor. In systemic analysis of action, the system is hardly ever static. The system of action is always a moving, dynamic system.

In analysing processes of change in the system of action, Parsons found it useful to take the idea of equilibrium as a point of departure. He has been much criticized for this. Critics saw it as evidence of an ideological bias towards social conservatism and the *status quo*. But it is only necessary to read Parsons attentively to see that he uses it only as a heuristic procedure. Parsons has often repeated that equilibrium is a limiting case, almost impossible to achieve in practice and scarcely ever corresponding to empirical reality. The equilibrium of which he speaks is a *theoretical point of reference* from which to begin the systemic analysis of action. Indeed, Parsons's conception of equilibrium inevitably calls for dynamic analysis, because the equilibrium to which he refers is *always problematic*. Equilibrium is disturbed the moment it is established. *In fact, action is a disequilibrating factor in a system tending towards but scarcely ever attaining equilibrium.* Every action calls forth a reaction, involving an endless chain of changes and readjustments. On several occasions, Parsons has invoked the principle that 'for every action there is an equal and opposite reaction'. By this he means that every action provokes a more or less equivalent reaction, and this reaction is itself an action which calls forth another reaction and so on.

A concrete example of a system of action in equilibrium would be an actor whose action conformed perfectly to what every other actor expected of him, and to the norms and values of the collectivity they formed together, and was at the same time entirely satisfying to the actor himself. It should be understood that such a situation would be quite exceptional, and that if it were to come about, it could exist for only a brief moment in time. But it is a sort of theoretical limiting case making possible a better appreciation of the permanent disequilibria in the actor/situation relationship, of the processes which cause them and the processes which they in turn trigger off.

Parsons adds that, as in physics, the hypothesis of equilibrium can be complemented with a 'law of inertia'. This is as follows : if no change affects a system of action, the system will continue indefinitely in a stable state. In other words, if a state of equilibrium comes about, theoretically it must persist unless and until some external disturbance intervenes. But in systems of action, as in physics, the law of inertia is theoretical, first because it assumes an equilibrium which is itself theoretical, and second because it presumes external conditions to be constant, though in practice they are continually changing.

What is it that is always disturbing equilibria and outwitting the law of inertia? According to Parsons, there are two main processes which modify the actor/situation relationship—*performance* and *learning*. Performance consists of all behaviour by which the actor disrupts his situation to a greater or lesser degree. At the same time, he is affected by the activities of other actors and by non-social objects in his environment (such as variations in temperature).

Learning is another form of change, which disrupts equilibria. What is learned and internalized generally has the effect of changing the actor, albeit slightly, and thus the conditions of his action and the action itself. The human actor is always assimilating new observations, new knowledge and ideas, and is always being modified by them, even if imperceptibly. These remarks about performance and learning apply to any actor, not only to individual actors but also to groups or collectivities taken as actors.

Further analysis of these two kinds of change reveals four others, according to whether the action in question is that of an actor or a system. To take the actor first, the two principal processes involved are *communication* and *decisions*. These two processes are involved in almost every one of an actor's actions. Moreover, every communication implies a decision as to what has to be communicated and as to the opportunity and necessity of communicating. By their very nature, both of these processes obviously disrupt equilibria, for they continually introduce new elements into a situation.

Turning to the system, Parsons sees a double process of change. On the one hand there is the process of *differentiation*, by which the parts of a system become more distinct, exhibiting individuality and relative autonomy, and fulfilling particular functions of their own. On the other hand, any system of action in which differentiation takes place must at the same time undergo a parallel process of *integration*; this links up the differentiated parts to each other, establishes bonds of interdependence and exchange, and connects them together so that they form a sufficiently co-ordinated whole. Parsons makes considerable use of the ideas of differentiation and integration.

2.8 The Cybernetic Hierarchy

Parsons's analysis of dynamic processes is rounded off by his borrowings from cybernetics, especially his conception of the cybernetic hierarchy (see Fig. 4). This is seen as an important principle

Functional dimensions of the system of action	Sub-systems of the system of action	Cybernetic relations
Pattern–maintenance	Cultural system	High information (Controls)
Integration	Social system	
Goal–attainment	Personality system	Hierarchy of conditions Hierarchy of controls
Adaptation	Organism	High energy (Conditions)

Fig. 4 Cybernetic Hierarchy and the General System of Action

both of integration and change.[16] Cybernetic theory led Parsons to assert that a system of action like all other functioning systems, living or otherwise, is characterized by a constant circulation of energy and information. It is exchanges of energy and information between its parts which stimulate the system into action. The parts of a system are not all equally endowed with information and energy; some have more energy, others more information at their command. Those which possess less energy benefit from more information, and *vice versa*. Now it is a fundamental principle of cybernetics that the parts which have high information impose controls on the high energy units. The result is that a hierarchically organized series of successive and cumulative controls is established in any system of action. At the base of the hierarchy are the parts highest in energy, acting as *factors conditioning action*; the high information units are at the top of the hierarchy, as *factors controlling action*.

Parsons claims that this principle is universally valid for any system of action. He often invokes it and, in his later writings, makes it one of the major rules of organization of systems of action. Returning to the four sub-systems of the general system of action, the organism can be identified as the sub-system highest in energy and lowest in information. Personality comes next, followed by the social system, while culture is obviously the sub-system most abundant in information and most lacking in energy. Between these four sub-systems, there is therefore established a hierarchy of controls, arranged in the order shown in Fig. 4. The result is that cultural elements, *in the last resort*, exercise control over the social system, personality and organism, whilst personality exerts control over the organism, but is subject to the more powerful controls stemming from the social system and culture.

The same principle applies to the four functional prerequisites. Among the categories of action, adaptation is much nearer to the source of energy, while pattern-maintenance, because of its link with culture, is much higher in information. Between the two, goal-attainment is nearer the high energy pole of the hierarchy while integration is nearer pattern-maintenance and high information. In any system of action, the hierarchy of controls begins with pattern-maintenance, followed by integration, goal-attainment and finally adaptation.

Finally, it must be emphasized that Parsons sees the cybernetic hierarchy as a principle of both order and change. It is a principle of order, because it governs the integration of the system's parts. And it is a principle of change, because it governs the direction in which conditioning and controlling factors operate.

NOTES

1. The elements of the general theory of action are scattered throughout Parsons's work. They are principally found in *The Structure of Social Action* (1937), *Toward a General Theory of Action* (1951), *Working Papers in the Theory of Action* (1953), and in a good number of articles, several of which will be mentioned in the course of this chapter.

2. Robert Bales, *Interaction Process Analysis* (Cambridge, Mass., Addison-Wesley, 1950).

3. Talcott Parsons, 'The Point of View of the Author', in *The Social Theories of Talcott Parsons: A Critical Examination*, edited by Max Black (Englewood Cliffs, NJ, Prentice-Hall, 1961) p 342.

4. Parsons discusses Tönnies's categories in a note at the end of chapter 17 of *The Structure of Social Action* (1937).

5. In most early formulations (*The Social System* (1951), *Toward a General Theory of Action* (1951)) Self-Orientation vs. Collectivity Orientation appears as the fifth pattern variable. This was later absorbed into the internal/external distinction implicit in the AGIL scheme (see below), Parsons also toyed with a sixth variable which was akin to the economic idea of 'rate of time preference' or 'time horizon' (see Parsons's 'Some comments on the State of the General Theory of Action', *American Sociological Review* **18** 6, 1953, pp 618–31. He subsequently decided that this variable was implicit in Affectivity/Affective Neutrality. (SJM)

6. 'The Professions and Social Structure', in *Social Forces* **17** 4, 1939, pp 457–67. Reprinted in *Essays in Sociological Theory* (1954).

7. *The Social System* (1951), chapter 10.

8. Parsons also describes the Quality vs. Performance choice as 'Ascription vs. Achievement', terms which he borrowed from Ralph Linton. Recruitment to many occupational roles in modern society is by achievement criteria, for which degrees, diplomas and certificates are taken as evidence. Crowns, however, are still passed on by ascriptive criteria, by preference to the eldest son of the monarch. (SJM)

9. For readers who, like me, find the word 'modality' impenetrably vague, Parsons and Shils explain that 'a modality is a property of an object; it is one of the aspects of an object in terms of which the object may be significant to the actor'. [*Toward a General Theory of Action* (1951), p 64.] (SJM)

10. 'Some Problems of General Theory in Sociology', in *Theoretical Sociology: Perspectives and Developments*, edited by J. C. McKinney and E. A. Tiryakian (New York, Appleton-Century-Crofts, 1970), p 29.

11. After *Working Papers* (1953), Parsons usually refers to this fourth function as *Pattern-Maintenance*, sometimes adding *and Tension-Management*. 'Latency' survives for the most part only as the 'L' in the abbreviation AGIL. (SJM)

12. Parsons usually presents his paradigms in simple property space and AGIL is always displayed in a four-cell box like that shown in Fig. 1.

13. Parsons's most detailed explanation of this is to be found in *Working Papers in the Theory of Action* (1953), chapters 3 and 5.

14. In 1960, Parsons refined his analysis of the relation between the pattern variables and the four functions still further in his article 'Pattern Variables Revisited: A Response to Robert Dubin', *American Sociological Review* **25** 4, 1960, pp 467–83. This article is reprinted in *Sociological Theory and Modern Society*, chapter 7.

15. P. A. Sorokin, *Society, Culture and Personality: Their Structure and Dynamics* (New York, Harper and Row, 1947).

16. Parsons explains his use of cybernetic theory in *Societies: Evolutionary and Comparative Perspectives* (1966), chapter 2.

3. Social System and Society

The previous chapter was devoted to presenting the general theory of action which is the kernel of Parsons's work. We have seen that Parsons intends the general theory of action as a very broad model at a sufficiently high level of generality to be applicable in all the sciences which focus on human action in one form or another. We can now turn to sociological theory proper. Parsons assigns a specific field of investigation to sociology. To define this, sociology has to be located within the general theory of action and in relation to the other social sciences.[1]

3.1 Sociology and the Social Sciences

Parsons defines the subject-matter of sociology as *social action specifically as embodied in social systems*. This means that since, within the framework of the system of action, the social system corresponds to the integration function, the latter is sociology's field of study. So, if the general system of action is taken as a point of departure, sociology is to be seen as distinguished from all the other social sciences by its specific field of enquiry.

As well as distinguishing sociology from the other social sciences, the general theory of action also pinpoints its relations with them. Human action as a whole spreads far beyond the social sub-system alone. It involves biological and neurological organisms, personalities, and a universe of symbols, norms and values. Only an 'encyclopaedic' discipline, as Parsons puts it, could cover every aspect of human action. But such a discipline would necessarily be imperialistic, because it would be an attempt to unify all knowledge concerning mankind within one conceptual or theoretical framework. From his earliest works, Parsons has rejected the claim that sociology, or for that matter any other discipline, is a sort of 'queen of the social sciences', enjoying a superior status and wider explanatory power than the others.

Parsons has always maintained a thoroughly egalitarian attitude to the various social sciences. Each of them—psychology, sociology, economics, political science and anthropology—deals with only one aspect of social action. None of these aspects is more fundamental than the others, for each is equally necessary to the understanding and explanation of concrete reality. So each discipline is a distinct science, while all of them together constitute the total science of action. An analytic distinction between the different disciplines is essential if confusion between the different aspects of action, to which the social sciences have too often been prone, is to be avoided. But at the same time, it must be said equally firmly that social action is an overall unity; analytically it can be divided, but concretely it is one. Consequently all the social sciences study what is concretely the same subject-matter, so there are always open boundaries between them. None of the social sciences can be self-contained, any more than it can predominate over the others.

To accord superior status to any one of the social sciences seems to Parsons to be a theoretical as well as methodological error. The parity between the various social sciences stems from each one's restricted perspective on human action, from their consequent complementarity, and from their being derived from the same conceptual framework. This is one of Talcott Parsons's most fundamental positions, and it pervades all his work—on psychology, economics and politics as well as sociology. Right at the beginning of his intellectual career, Parsons took up this position, à propos not sociology but economics. One of the major problems dealt with in his first articles published betwen 1928 and 1935, and in his doctoral thesis at Heidelberg, concerned the non-economic aspects of economic processes which economists have tended to treat as marginal to their discipline. In the eighteenth and nineteenth centuries political economy might have become the encyclopaedic social science. However, it failed to do so because classical economics explicitly chose to concern itself with only one kind of human action, rational economic behaviour. Anything which did not meet certain criteria of rationality was not considered relevant; classical economic theory strove to keep such matters outside its field of investigation, taking it as axiomatic that whatever did not lend support to its argument could be treated as 'constant'.

Parsons was convinced that the same reasoning should apply to the other social sciences. Each of them ought to follow the example of economics and avoid the temptation to be encyclopaedic, devoting itself instead to analysing one particular aspect of human action. Each would then acquire a clear identity and well-defined boundaries, as did economics.

On the other hand, classical economics fell into the error of declaring everything marginal to its own field to be constant, and then proceeding to ignore it. This attitude could be defended when economics was virtually the only social science, but it has become untenable today. While maintaining the autonomy of each of the social sciences, the links uniting them need to be systematically explored. This can only be done if there is an accepted common denominator of all the social sciences; and that is what Parsons put forward in the general theory of action.

3.2 Social Interaction

We have already said that, according to Parsons, the subject-matter of sociology is social action as it is embodied in social systems. This calls for explanation. What is distinctive about this particular form of social action?

A social system is first and foremost a network of relationships between people and between groups; it links together a plurality of actors. In other words, *actors' actions in a social system are considered specifically from the point of view of their interaction with other actors.* In this perspective, physical and symbolic or cultural objects do not, strictly speaking, belong to the social system : they become external factors conditioning or determining interaction between actors.

It should be noted immediately that the actors in social systems are not necessarily just individual people. They may also be groups or collectivities, such as a village, a region, a social class or a nation. So the application of the Parsonian interaction schema is not confined to the level of interpersonal relations alone, but can be extended to all levels of social reality.

Social interaction involves three elements. First there must be reciprocal expectations between actors. A particular actor, 'Ego' expects the other actor or actors, represented here by 'Alter', to behave in such and such a way, given their common circumstances and relationship with each other. At the same time, Ego knows that Alter for his part also has expectations relating to the same situation. Second, there must be norms and values, which govern or are supposed to govern actors' behaviour. Indeed, reciprocal expectations exist because of norms and values. It does not matter very much whether Ego and Alter refer to the same norms or to different ones; the essential thing is that Ego knows which norms guide Alter and that Alter knows which norms guide Ego. This makes possible Ego's expectation that Alter will behave in such and such a way, because from known rules of conduct he can predict that Alter ought to act in a certain way in a given situation. Lastly sanctions are the third element contributing to interaction. Ego and Alter 'reward' and 'punish' each other, according to whether the other conforms or does not conform to expectations.

Parsons sees these three elements—expectations, norms and sanctions—as the components of *roles*. Parsons drew the concept of role from the American social scientific tradition, especially from American sociology, anthropology and social psychology. George Herbert Mead in particular made it a key idea in his analysis of the relations between the individual and society, and this partly explains the abundant use of it by American sociologists of all schools of thought. Transposed into Parsonian sociology, the role concept relates to *an institutionalized definition, explicit or implicit, of expectations, norms and sanctions which condition the behaviour of an actor in consequence of the position he occupies in the social structure.* For example, there are expectations, norms and sanctions concerning the behaviour of anyone occupying the position of father in any given society.

For Parsons, it is always in and through a role that Ego is in interaction with other actors, who are themselves also in interaction with him in and through roles. Interaction necessarily implies actors-in-roles, because it is only by and through roles that it is possible for actors to enter into relationships with each other. What is called an institution—for instance the family, school or factory—is nothing but a complex of complementary and co-ordinated roles.

Parsons describes this interdependence of roles as a situation of 'double contingency'. Ego's behaviour depends on what he thinks Alter is expecting from him, and on the sanctions which Alter, for his part, can bring to bear. At the same time, Alter's behaviour is also conditioned by what he thinks Ego is expecting him to do. In an extreme case, double contingency might produce complete deadlock between Ego and Alter, were it not precisely for roles defining expectations and making them explicit, thereby making double contingency a principle of action rather than inaction.

Lastly, it should be emphasized that interaction, as it is conceived by Parsons, is essentially an exchange. It is an exchange of information about reciprocal expectations; also an exchange of sanctions and therefore of gratifications and frustrations. The idea of interaction as exchange at every level of the social system where interaction takes place, is very important in Parsonian sociology, as will be seen.

3.3 The Social System and its Environment

Interaction is what distinguishes the social system from the other sub-systems of action. Artificially abstracted from the rest of the system of action, the social system is a theoretical entity constituted by the interaction among members of a collectivity.

In this context, Parsons makes a point which is central to his theory : for each of the sub-systems, the three others comprise what he calls its environment. So each sub-system interacts and has exchange relations with each of the other three. All of them are bound together in a network of interdependence, though each remains sufficiently autonomous to be analytically distinguishable from the rest. Consequently it is possible to analyse any system of action from five different points of reference. First, the system of action itself can be taken as the point of reference; the four sub-systems are then defined as categories into which its constituents can be differentiated. Second, each of the four sub-systems in turn can be taken as the system of reference. In each case, the three other sub-systems represent the environment of the one taken as the point of reference.

The social system, as has been said, corresponds to the integration function in the general theory of action. It is that aspect of a system of action which includes the interactional links between member units, as well as the exigencies of communication and co-ordination which arise from complex patterns of interaction. And it includes the efforts which every system of action makes to create and maintain solidarity and loyalty, to minimize conflicts and discourage deviance. In other words, in the social system the emphasis is on factors which bring together, unite and regulate the elements of a system of action.

For the social system, the behavioural organism is the meeting point of, on the one hand, the physical and biological resources necessary to action and, on the other hand, the system of action itself. The senses obviously mediate relations between the system of action and the physical environment, giving the latter meaning or utility for the system of action. More precisely, the organism contributes directly to the production and consumption of benefits or goods and to their transformation into energy useful to the system of action. That is why work is so important, as well as technology, which has so extended and amplified the scope of human activity. For the social system, the organic system is therefore the means of access to the material, physical, geographical, biological and technical environment.

The personality system is central to the motivation necessary for the social system. In effect, what the social system requires from the personality system is a collection of dispositions and inclinations leading the subject-actors towards behaviour favourable to the interests of the system—towards sociability, solidarity, and the internalization of norms, values and ideologies. This motivation is not generated within the social system itself, as defined by Parsons; it is drawn from the very fabric of the personality systems of the actors participating in the social system.

Finally, the cultural system provides the social system with what Parsons calls legitimation. Through the cultural system, the social system derives values and norms which help to create solidarity, loyalty and control, and ensure that the social system is at least relatively stable through time.

There is no space to deal further with this set of interrelations. Suffice it to say that they are the basis of Parsons's fundamental postulate about the complementarity of socialization and institu-tionalization; they lead to the interpenetration of the psychological and social, and to the unity of the system of action as a whole.

3.4 A Distinction of Levels

The same mode of analysis into four sub-systems can also be applied to the internal organization of the social system. The social system should now no longer be thought of as a sub-system but as a system of action containing in turn four sub-systems corresponding to adaptation, goal-attainment, integration and pattern-maintenance. However, when Parsons reaches this point, he finds it more useful to *change the level of analysis. Instead of the social system, he takes a society as his unit for analysis, and it is the society which he dissects into sub-systems.* This is an important distinction and must not be overlooked.

In fact, the title of this chapter, 'Social system and society', is not a pleonasm; there is nothing redundant about it. In contrast to many sociologists who use the two terms interchangeably, Parsons maintains a clear distinction between a social system and a society, a distinction which has become fundamental to Parsonian sociology. Failure to be aware of and understand this distinction makes many passages in Parsons's writings seem obscure or contradictory.

For Parsons, the concept of social system has a specific and well-defined meaning. It is the whole web of interaction through which two or more actors are related to each other, influence each other and act collectively in every way possible. Thus defined, the concept of social system is a tool of analysis; it represents a way of perceiving reality but it is not the conceptual counterpart of some concrete reality. It exists on an exclusively abstract and analytical plane; it is a category of the general theory of action. Parsons's social system is at the same level of abstraction as the general system of action, since it is one of its components. It is an idea of which he makes analytic and heuristic use.

One of the essential postulates of Parsonian theory is that the concept of social system can be used in analysing groups, collectivities, institutions, associations and movements of every shape and size. An industrial enterprise, a university, a social class, a whole society—all these can be analysed as social systems.

In contradistinction to the concept of a social system, that of society refers to concrete realities. When Parsons speaks of a society, he means an actual collectivity that can be identified, located and delimited. More exactly, a society is a relatively self-sufficient collectivity the members of which are able to satisfy all their individual and collective needs and to live entirely within its framework. Empirically, a society may be a country or nation, and sometimes even an empire or civilization. But it should be remembered that in Parsons's work, neither the concept of society nor that of social system includes culture. Many sociologists use the term society to refer to the symbolic and normative sphere as well as to social interaction and social institutions. Parsons uses both social system and society to refer only to the latter.

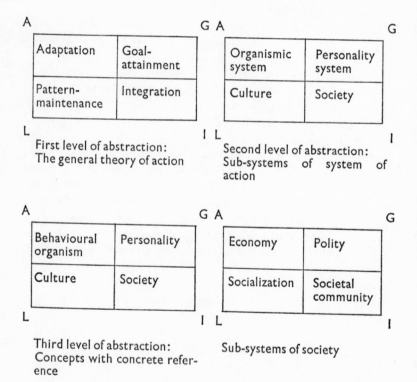

Fig. 5 Three Levels of Abstraction and the Sub-systems of Society[2]

SOCIAL SYSTEM AND SOCIETY 61

It can be seen that Parsons distinguishes three levels of abstraction. The first is that of the conceptual scheme of the general theory of action, with its four functional sub-systems : adaptation, goal-attainment, integration and latency or pattern-maintenance. This is the most abstract and general level because it is applicable to any system of action of any kind. The second level is that at which Parsons distinguishes four sub-systems within the system of action : the behavioural organism, the personality system, the social system and the cultural system. Finally, the third level of analysis is that of concepts corresponding to concrete reality. This is the case with the notion of society which, as we shall see, can in its turn be divided into sub-systems. Figure 5 summarizes these three levels in the usual paradigm. It also shows Parsons's analysis of the internal organization and functions of a society, which is what will be discussed next.

3.5 The Sub-systems of Society

The internal organization of a society can be analysed into four sub-systems, according to the model of the system of action. But though the sub-systems are derived analytically, they correspond with aspects of reality. In a society, adaptation corresponds to the complex of activities concerned with production and distribution. Labour is the principal means by which a society is related to its environment, and seeks to survive in it, use it and benefit by it. So in the context of a total society, adaptation corresponds to all activities constituting the *economy* or economic sub-system. In Parson's usage, the economic function is not confined only to strictly economic structures and institutions, though it is concentrated mainly in these.

Goal-attainment in a society becomes the pursuit of collective objectives and the mobilization of the society's actors and resources to achieve these objectives. Parsons calls this the *polity*. It must be stressed that he uses this term in a very general sense to mean all forms of decision-making and mobilization of resources. In this sense the polity is not confined to the institutions of the state, but extends into businesses, administration, and social and political movements.

The complex of processes by which the *socialization* of members is accomplished represents the pattern-maintenance function in society. Through socialization, culture is transmitted to actors, internalized by them, and becomes an important factor in the motivation of their social behaviour. This function is largely concentrated in the family and the educational system, although the mass media, trade unions and political parties also have an educational role.

Finally, to the integration function within a society, Parsons gives the name of the *societal community*. This includes the complex of institutions which function to establish and maintain the interdependencies societies require between their members. These are the institutions which establish the patterns of co-ordination necessary to the working of society if there is not to be too much chaos and conflict. The societal community is the sphere of social control, but it is as much a source of consent as of coercion. In its most structured form, the societal community is represented by law and judicial institutions, and in its least structured by various kinds of solidarity and feelings of fellowship.

3.6 The Societal Community

These distinctions help to clarify exactly what Parsons sees as sociology's field of investigation. From the point of view of the general theory of action, sociology's area of study is the integrative function. And within a society, it is the same, for the societal community is the integrative aspect of society.

According to Parsons, each of the four sub-systems of society corresponds to a particular social scientific discipline. Economics studies the adaptive sub-system, and political science goal-attainment. Pattern-maintenance falls to psychology either in general or specifically to social psychology, and perhaps also to anthropology. It can be seen that pattern-maintenance in particular poses problems for Parsons, for he is not quite sure to which discipline it should be assigned. But Parsons has a clear view of sociology; it is the study of the societal community sub-system. It does not deal with every aspect of society; if it did, it would straddle economics, poltical science, social psychology and anthropology and that would run counter to the Parsonian principle of the parity of the social sciences. Parsons maintains that only one aspect of society justifies the separate existence of sociology as a science—integration, or the societal community.

Sometimes,[3] Parsons has seemed to link the societal community to Durkheim's idea of solidarity, and to the two types of solidarity—mechanical and organic—which he distinguished. In fact, the societal community consists of all the links which promote solidarity, binding together the members of society and making them dependent on one another, giving at least relative cohesion to the complex which they collectively form. This definition of sociology and its subject-matter places Parsons perhaps more than any other contemporary sociologist in the Durkheimian tradition. More concretely, by societal community, Parsons means the institutions, social classes, organizations, social movements, pressure groups and so on which draw members of society together and through which they defend their interests, satisfy their needs and realize their ends.

In a society as in any system of action, the sub-systems are at once autonomous and interdependent, so that the disciplines related to them are also independent of each other, yet interrelated. It is possible and even necessary to distinguish the various social sciences, but at the same time there are links between them which must never be forgotten or neglected.

It has been seen here how Parsons is finally led to a much more restricted view of sociology than the majority of European and American sociologists. No one has taken more seriously than Parsons the need to resolve the confusion between the social sciences. At the same time he also insists more than any other sociologist on the unity of the social sciences and the essential links between them.

3.7 Systems of Exchange

As a system of action, the societal community studied by sociologists enjoys relative autonomy; it constantly maintains a network of boundaries distinguishing it from environing systems. At the same time, the societal community is also an open system interacting with its environment. It is in continual communication with the three other systems which make up its immediate environment: the economy, the polity and the institutions of socialization. There is a complex network of exchanges between each of these four systems.

Parsons draws particular attention to two aspects which he considers essential to this network of exchanges. First, inspired by economic theory and especially by Leontief's work, Parsons believes it possible to represent the exchanges between each pair of systems in terms of an 'input–output table'. Every system receives, from each of the other three, things essential to its functioning (inputs); in return it offers them the 'products' of its own activities (outputs). Parsons pushes this analogy with economic exchanges still further; according to him there is always a double exchange between any two systems : an exchange of *factors of production* (inputs) and an exchange of *products* (outputs). So each sub-system in society is like a firm specializing in the production of activities in response to certain specific needs, creating a kind of market in which each sub-system exchanges its own products for those of other systems.

Second, Parsons underlines the theoretical importance of media of exchange for a system of this kind. Such a system cannot exist without symbols facilitating communication and exchange. As each sub-system is involved in a network of exchanges, Parsons concluded that four media of exchange must exist, each based on one of the four sub-systems. Economic analysis was again Parsons's inspiration in developing his scheme of four media of exchange. *Money* serves as his model, since its functions as a medium of exchange have been fully studied by economists. But Parsons put the economists' analysis in a new and original perspective. First he defined money as the link between the economy and society; the former becomes a sub-system of the latter thanks to the network of exchanges which money enables it to carry on with the other sub-systems of society. Parsons also emphasizes the symbolic nature of money, which makes it resemble a language. Money states the value of a thing or service; it calls for a reply expressed in monetary terms. So Parsons came to see the whole monetary system as a code, the rules of which regulate the circulation of goods and services.

It was while working on economic sociology that Parsons began to perceive the various symbolic aspects of money and its functions in the interaction between the economy and the other sub-systems of society. From this, Parsons concluded that a medium of exchange must logically be found in each of the three other sub-systems, fulfilling functions analogous to money. Whence his scheme of four media of exchange.

Within the polity, the equivalent of money seems to Parsons to be *power*. Parsons defines power as *the capacity to compel a society's actors to fulfil the obligations imposed on them by collective goals, so that the society's resources can be mobilized to attain the designated ends.*[4] So defined, power is something quite different from authority. Parsons sees authority as a property of certain positions to which power accumulates; the holder of a position of authority gains an amount of power which he can use and pass into circulation. Authority itself does not circulate; it is 'the institutionalized code defining rights of participation in the power system'.[5] On the other hand, power in Parsons's sense is neither fixed nor stable. Rather it is a means of exchange which, like money, has a symbolic value with a code of its own, and it circulates from the polity in the exchanges between the subsystems.

The third medium of exchange Parsons calls *influence*. This has its origin in the integrative system, the societal community. Influence is *the capacity to obtain consent, approval or loyalty by the exercise of persuasion.* It differs from power in that it is not a form of compulsion and it does not justify any resort to force. Influence is rather linked to the prestige of whoever wields it, or to his ability to make some sort of appeal for solidarity. As with money and power, influence is essentially mobile, in that it facilitates exchange through which it moves and circulates. Like money and power it can also increase and diminish according to the use made of it by the individuals of groups who gain it.

The last medium of exchange is what Parsons calls *commitments* to values and norms. It is through these commitments that cultural ingredients are transposed into social reality and enter the circuit of exchange relationships. Each actor can theoretically be considered to acquire 'commitments' to conform to certain norms and values of a particular culture. That is how he is recognized as belonging to a given society, and how he himself recognizes his belonging. Having acquired these commitments which integrate him into society he can, so to speak, use them as security to obtain what he needs or desires of the influence, power and money circulating in society.

The function of these four media of exchange is to ensure the continual circulation within society of what Parsons calls 'resources' —of both the 'factors of production' and the 'products' of each of the four sub-systems. The great complex of exchanges is summarized in Fig. 6. This shows a double interchange (represented by four arrows) between each of the sub-systems: an exchange of factors of production in both directions and an exchange of products also in both directions. Parsons calls each of the six double interchanges a 'system of exchange'. It is possible to spell out more exactly what is exchanged between each pair of sub-systems. Each

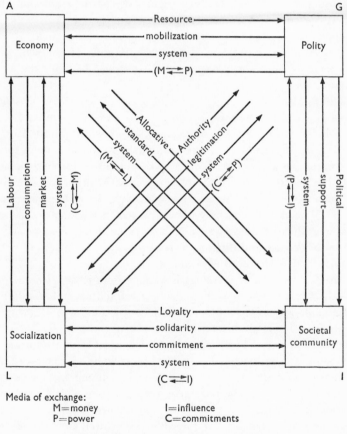

Media of exchange:
M=money   I=influence
P=power   C=commitments

Fig. 6 Systems of Exchange in Society

double interchange involves both an exchange of the two media of exchange originating in the two sub-systems concerned, and also an exchange of the products of the respective sub-systems. Thus, to take an example from Fig. 6, consider what Parsons calls the 'resource mobilization system'. The polity (which is much wider than the state alone) uses its stocks of power in a great many ways to maintain and increase the productivity of the economy. In return it receives the goods and services produced by the economy and has a hand in allocating them between individuals and groups in society. It would take too long to explain each of the other five systems of exchange in Fig. 6, but they will be discussed in more detail in the next chapter.[6]

Parsons discusses this vast ring of interaction and exchange under the heading of 'the dynamics of social equilibrium'.[7] By using this seemingly paradoxical expression, Parsons meant to stress that just like the systems of action discussed in the last chapter, a society is a living, moving, changing thing. Change is as much a part of its nature as interaction. In this context change takes two forms : the exchanges themselves, and the endless chain of adaptation and readaptation consequent on the disturbances accompanying the exchanges. It is theoretically possible to conceive of a social system without any disturbances; it would need to attain a perfect balance in all six systems of exchange. But in practice that is nearly impossible, because the exchanges almost inevitably introduce modifications or disturbances in one or other of the structural systems. It can be seen that equilibrium, as Parsons uses the idea here, is something neither real nor desired. It is simply a heuristic device, a theoretical reference point, useful in interpreting changes within systems of action.

3.8 Structural Change

It is, however, necessary to distinguish between change *within* and change *of* a social system. The processes described as 'the dynamics of social equilibrium' are not really substantial changes. They are ways in which any society functions without necessarily undergoing changes of structure. So these dynamics must not be confused with social change. In Parsonian sociology, social change proper appears in two forms : in the form of what Parsons calls structural changes, and in the form of long-term evolution.

Structural changes are important changes in the organization and functioning of a society, or a sub-structure or sub-system of a society, by which they move from one social type or category to another. Examples are the transformation of a traditional society into an industrial society, feudal to bourgeois society, capitalist to socialist society.

What are the *sources* of structural change? Parsons finds it useful to distinguish sources of change external to society from those which are internal. Exogenous factors can be of various kinds. Genetic modifications of the organism, variations in the physical environment or climate, and technological changes may be mentioned. For example, in his analysis of the division of labour, Durkheim cited the influence of demographic factors on what he called moral density which in turn was a factor favourable to the division of labour.

Sociologists have, however, too readily limited exogenous sources of change to those of the kind just mentioned. Parsons adds that for any given system, it is also necessary to consider as exogenous factors changes originating in other environing systems. For example, on the micro-sociological plane, changes which befall the personality can naturally affect the social system. Or again, variations in the cultural universe of values and symbols can have an influence on a society, even if these cultural changes do not originate in that society.

Endogenous factors are more difficult to circumscribe and list than exogenous ones. Of the endogenous factors, Parsons attributes particular importance to the role played by strains in society. Strains are internal difficulties, contradictions, frictions and maladjustments which make the system's functioning more troublesome, difficult, and sometimes less effective. There are always strains in every society and they have a positive value in that they are sources of action and innovation. But it sometimes happens that strains find no means of expressing themselves. So a reservoir of tensions builds up, and strains cannot be relieved in any positive way. Overfilling this reservoir tends in the end to bring on structural change of greater or lesser violence.

Strain often appears to be an internal reaction to exogenous sources of change. It is generally through the internal strains they provoke that exogenous factors contribute to social change. For example technological change leads to maladjustments in the organization of work, setting up strains which in turn call forth structural change. Strain serves in some ways to transmit the influence of exogenous factors, often also amplifying it and extending its range through time.

Exogenous and endogenous factors do not, however, in themselves bring about change. Sometimes they are present, yet no changes occur. That is because the forces for change in society remain weaker than the forces maintaining equilibrium, the forces of social control. Certain *conditions* must be fulfilled for the balance to be swung the other way. First, the strain within society must be strong enough to engender and maintain the motivation necessary to bring about change. Second, effective machinery must be developed for destroying or evading the resistance of those who have a vested interest in maintaining the *status quo*. Otherwise there is a risk that, in the face of the forces of control, strain will create only passivity or indirect and ineffective forms of hostility. Third, it is necessary that a clear, realistic and realizable model of a new society appears. Without such a model, the forces of change risk quick exhaustion without producing any effective action. Fourth, a new complex of sanctions must progressively appear, rewarding new behaviour in accordance with new norms, and tending to destroy the old.

Parsons adds one last condition : the forces of change must reach up to as high a rung as possible in the cybernetic hierarchy, normally at the level of symbols and values. It is there that the most powerful forces of control are located. Consequently, if the strains do not reach the universe of values and the latter are untouched by the forces of change, it is likely that resistance to change will gain momentum. The new sanctions and models of society must draw their inspiration from the realm of values just as the old ones did.

Structural change remains only one of the possible responses to rising strains in society. If the conditions favourable to change are not fulfilled, society finds other ways of eliminating them. Forces of control can sometimes succeed in resolving tensions by simple processes of equilibration—the existing state of affairs is modified sufficiently to weaken the impact of the forces of change very greatly. A second possibility is that though the forces of change are stifled, they may reappear in other forms and sometimes with increased strength. It is also possible for forces of change to be isolated and made harmless to the rest of the system—they may, so to speak, be shunted into a siding. Finally, if the strains are too strong yet do not bring about the desired changes, the society may end up by disappearing as an autonomous entity, becoming disorganized, merging with or being conquered by another society.

This, in brief summary, is how Parsons approaches social change. He does not give it as central a position in his theory as many of his critics would like, but it would be unfair to say that he has completely neglected social change. And in his most recent work, Parsons has developed a strongly neo-evolutionist approach. For him, long-term evolution is simply another form of structural change.

3.9 The Evolution of Societies

Parsons follows in the tradition of the founding fathers of sociology —among them Durkheim, Spencer, Weber, Sombart and Marx— whose approach was generally evolutionary or historical. Under their influence, he came to consider the problem of the evolution of societies through the ages, the phases through which civilizations pass, and the great sweeping movements of history. But it was also through his contact with them that Parsons became convinced that their work had been premature, because they did not have the theoretical and conceptual framework which would have enabled them to disentangle the great trends of history and the principal stages of human and social evolution. Parsons believes that with the theoretical scheme he elaborated in his earlier work, he is now better equipped to reconsider the evolutionary theses of the founding fathers.

Parsons explains evolution by means of two main laws : a general law of evolution, which specifies the principle involved; and the law of cybernetic hierarchy, which indicates the direction of evolution. He takes his general law of evolution from biology, which of all sciences relating to man has gone furthest in analysing evolution and its causes. It was in biology that evolutionary theories were most highly developed in the nineteenth century, and in comparison with the social sciences, biology has maintained its progress in this field. In Parsons's view, there is no difficulty in borrowing the general law of evolution from biology, for there are certain common denominators between the principles of evolution and those of the general theory of action. In particular, in social history as well as in the history of living organisms, systems which have survived and become the most developed have shown greater ability than others for adapting to their environment and changes within it. The capacity for adaptation is one of the great principles of all forms of life, whether animal, vegetable, psychological or social. A system, of whatever kind it may be, survives, develops and progresses to the extent that it retains the capacity to readapt continually to its environment and to new situations. The fundamental principle of evolution is *the capacity for generalized adaptation.*

In its turn, this capacity for adaptation boils down to two great processes underlying all change—differentiation and integration. Growing structural differentiation enables a society to respond fully to all its needs. At the same time, because it is becoming more differentiated, a society has to invent new modes of integration in order to co-ordinate the new and more numerous parts of which it is composed. Increasing differentiation, accompanied by sustained integration, gives a society the adaptability necessary to evolve according to its needs and the exigencies of its environment.

We have already encountered the second law—the principle of *cybernetic hierarchy.* This tells us that in long-term social evolution over several generations, changes in the cultural system are the most important. Because culture comes first in the hierarchy of control, it has a dominant influence over the social and other systems. Changes at this level are likely to affect society deeply and for long periods.

With these two laws, Parsons distinguishes three principal stages in social evolution : primitive societies, intermediate societies and modern societies.[8] In accordance with the principle of the cybernetic hierarchy, the three types of society are distinguished by a cultural criterion. The transition from primitive to intermediate society is marked by the appearance of *writing.* This represents a very important revolution for it strongly helps to stabilize the cultural sphere. Once language is written, more rigorous grammatical codes and syntax can develop, and vocabulary becomes endlessly richer. Writing also allows events, ideas, feelings and emotions to be crystallized or objectified. Thanks to writing, man can objectify his thought, projecting it outside himself, and make it a sort of raw material to be worked upon. Similarly, writing enables human societies to look back at their history. Oral tradition could only keep memories alive for a few generations; archives extend the historical perspective indefinitely. In short, with writing, culture became more stable and broke away from the everyday communication on which it had hitherto been entirely dependent. Thus culture was able to become more autonomous from events, less dependent on chance circumstances, and more a system in itself. Writing brings about a clearer differentiation between culture and the other systems of action, and this, Parsons claims, can only be a sign of development.

The transition from intermediate to modern society was marked by the appearance of *law* and judicial institutions like courts and strict rules of procedure. Law, too, helped culture to become more stable and permanent. Law rigorously defines rules and norms of behaviour, specifies concrete applications of general values, and institutionalizes principles, ideas and ideals. With the advent of law, customs become less subject to short-term influences, less bound to the chance of passing events. When jurisprudence appears and law becomes codified, culture is expressed more rigorously in written rules. Officials are then needed to interpret the rules, but at the same time they are themselves bound by them.

Thus, for Parsons social evolution takes the form of the progressive strengthening of culture in human social life; it is bound up with progress towards a more differentiated and at the same time more stable cultural system with a richer, expanded and diversified content.

But has Parsons made too limited a use of his idea of cybernetic hierarchy? He uses only the hierarchy of controls and leaves out the hierarchy of conditioning factors. Taken as a whole, allowing for the 'upward' effects of conditions as well as the 'downward' effects of controls, the cybernetic idea would probably provide Parsons with a more complex model, capable of encompassing more features of reality. As he presents it, Parsons's evolutionary theory comes strangely close to Spencer's; Parsons does not appear to have made an original contribution to social evolutionism.

However, Parsons's evolutionary theory does throw light on his whole sociology. It is evident—as Parsons himself has stressed many times—that Parsonian sociology is mainly concerned with complex societies, the most advanced societies in terms of social evolution. In fact, Parsons's theoretical framework applies best to highly differentiated societies, in which the distinctions between culture and social system, between religion and politics, between economy and polity, between law and morals are very clearly developed. The paradigm of differentiation was inspired by the analysis of complex societies and applies above all to them.

Parsons considers that sociological theory can only develop within advanced societies, where the sub-systems are sufficiently differentiated for them to be analysed. Parsons's conceptual and theoretical scheme has been criticized on the ground that it is not applicable to primitive societies and is therefore not universal in scope. But in Parsons's view, this is simply evidence that advanced societies provide the main object for sociological thought and analysis.

3.10 Comparative Sociology

For Parsons, evolutionism is the basis for comparative sociology. He is convinced that societies cannot be compared unless they are located on an evolutionary scale, making it possible to describe one society as more 'advanced' than another. An evolutionary scale of development through time establishes the criteria for comparisons between societies.

Comparative sociology poses two methodological problems. First, it has to be decided which structures or aspects of one society it is important to compare with which aspects of another. In other words, which aspects theoretically correspond to each other and which *similarities* are theoretically significant? Second, it is equally necessary to be able to assess the importance of *differences* observed in the structures of two or more societies. An evolutionary perspective on societies solves this double problem by indicating which components are transformed in the course of history and the principal stages in the evolution of societies. This makes it possible to find points of comparison between societies at quite different stages of the evolutionary process.

This link between comparative sociology and evolutionism is very important to Parsons, because he considers that comparative studies are essential to the scientific character of social science. Comparison of societies or collectivities is the equivalent in the social sciences of laboratory experiment in the natural sciences. A sociologist comparing societies from different periods and areas of the globe can vary certain factors while holding others constant, just like a scientist in his laboratory. Manipulation of variables is rarely possible in the social sciences, but comparative studies allow it in an indirect way.

The conceptual scheme so far outlined is useful for purposes of comparative sociology in three ways. First of all, the principle of differentiation provides some important benchmarks. A more differentiated society is one which is structurally and functionally more advanced in the general scheme of development. Consequently the more a society shows marked differentiation between its four sub-systems, the more can it be said to be advanced in comparison with others from the point of view of overall development. So the four sub-system paradigm is an essential reference point for comparative sociology. It means that sociologists need be neither arbitrary nor imprecise in comparing societies. They can make reference to an analytical scheme applicable to any social system or collectivity. The paradigm's high level of abstraction warrants its very general use for purposes of comparative research.

Second, in any concrete system of action, the four sub-systems are not of equal importance. One sub-system is often more prominent in one society than in another. For example in industrial societies, the economic function has developed and proliferated to the extent that it has overall primacy in society; specialized institutions appear with the sole function of producing and distributing goods. In contrast, there are examples of societies in which the political function became predominant and pervaded the whole social system. This was particularly true of ancient Egyptian society, which came to revolve entirely about the bureaucratic governmental administration over which the Pharoah presided. Parsons himself has not elaborated a great deal on the paradigm of differentiation for comparative purposes. But he has said enough to suggest its possibilities, especially in relation to industrial society.

The third feature of Parsons's conceptual scheme useful for comparative studies is the pattern variables. Here Parsons has been more explicit. He devoted several pages in *The Social System* to showing how the two variables particularism/universalism and quality/performance could be used as a general framework for comparative analysis. As Fig. 7 shows, these two variables form a classification of four different types of society, of which Parsons gives concrete illustrations. And this typology identifies four principal classes of society which can be traced through history.[9]

Using the pattern variables like this in a comparative and evolutionary perspective, Parsons in effect comes full circle. By way of comparative sociology, evolutionism leads back to the starting point of the theory of action, the pattern variables, which are the fundamental structural categories of any system of action. Structural analysis is integrated with dynamic analysis. So there is a

	Universalism	Particularism
Performance	Societies placing high value on personal achievement, through rules which are applied irrespective of the people concerned (e.g. the USA).	Societies placing high value on personal achievement, in accordance with rules which take account of the particular relational context in which the actor is involved (e.g. classical China).
Quality	Societies in which action is guided by universalistic norms, but where the traditional status hierarchy remains predominantly important within the social system (e.g. Germany).	Societies in which action is guided by norms which vary according to the status of the actor and to the particular context of the action (e.g. Latin America).

Fig. 7 Types of Society Classified According to Two of the Pattern Variables

unity in the theoretical model which Parsons intended it to have from the start. But it remains to be asked how far this intention was carried out effectively, and at what cost.

NOTES

1. The exposition of Parsons's specifically *sociological* theory is mainly to be found in the following works: *Essays in Sociological Theory* (1949; 2nd edn 1954), *The Social System* (1951), *Structure and Process in Modern Societies* (1960), *Theories of Society* (1961), and *Sociological Theory and Modern Society* (1967).
2. This is a considerably re-drawn version of Rocher's Fig. 5. (SJM)
3. Especially in his article 'Systems Analysis: Social Systems' in the *International Encyclopaedia of the Social Sciences* (New York: The MacMillan Company and The Free Press, 1968) pp 458–73.
4. This is a translation of Rocher's paraphrase of Parsons, and is perhaps a little clearer than Parsons's original. Parsons's actual words are quoted on p 90 below. (SJM)
5. Here we have slightly added to Rocher's text, drawing directly on *Politics and Social Structure* (1969), pp 371–3. (SJM)
6. They are set out in full in *Politics and Social Structure*, p 399. (SJM)
7. 'An Outline of the Social System', in *Theories of Society* (1961), vol 1, p 60.
8. Parsons sets out the three stages in two books: *Societies: Evolutionary and Comparative Perspectives* (1966) and *The System of Modern Societies* (1971). The latter deals with the third stage, but appeared too late to be included in this analysis.
9. Talcott Parsons, *The Social System* (1951), pp 102, 180–200.

4. The Economic and Political Systems

A theory as general and comprehensive as Parsons's spreads in all directions and it has come to include economics and political science within its area of analysis. In fact, the economy and polity are the other two 'active' sub-systems of society, and they are closely inter-related with the societal community sub-system. It was logical that after Parsons had elaborated his general theory of action, he would want to try to apply it in studying the economic and political systems.

The evolution of Parsons's thought did not, however, really follow such a clear course. What appears *a posteriori* as a new development had in fact been present from the start. Economic theory had been one of Parsons's major starting points. Indeed his idea of social action was largely inspired by his analyses of economic action. In his first works, Parsons discussed Marshall's model of economic behaviour at some length, and this led him to extend it later, with modifications, to the whole of social action. In the development of Parsons's thought, social man was first an extension of economic man; later economic man became an aspect of social man.

Further, in the course of the development of the general theory of action, economics supplied Parsons with certain key concepts of which he has made extensive use. In particular, economic ideas helped him to construct his table of interaction and exchange between systems of action. The influence of economics no doubt explains why Parsons sees society as a vast market in which exchange takes place between individual and collective units, and in which not only money but power, influence and commitments circulate.

A chronological account of the development of Parsons's thought would have to start with his economic sociology. He was made aware of the limitations of an exclusively economic approach to economic problems by reading Weber and through working on his

77

doctoral thesis at Heidelberg. This led him to want to show that the economy is a sector of society and has to be analysed as such, and that in refusing to consider the interaction between the phenomena they study and the rest of society, economists were narrowing their field of vision excessively. But in order to study that interaction, a general theory had to be developed which was capable of over-arching both the economy and the other sub-systems of society. And his theoretical strategy in developing his system led Parsons to postulate that a general theory of action should be applicable to all the social sciences, including political science as well as economics.

The importance of this chapter in understanding Parsons's thought requires no further comment. Economic sociology is central to the Parsonian scheme. And political sociology is the principal field into which Parsons has transposed the general model of social analysis which he borrowed from economics.

4.1 The Economic System

One of the principal traits—if not *the* principal trait—of modern industrial societies as Parsons sees them is the predominance of economic activity and institutions. Compared with primitive and intermediate societies, modern societies have witnessed great growth in the world of production, the occupational sphere, the network of monetary transactions, and in the importance of credit. Modern industrial society—and especially, Parsons believes, modern capitalist society—is the place *par excellence* to study the economy and its place within society. It is in this type of society that the economy is most differentiated from the rest of social activity; it is an easily identifiable sub-system and its interactions and interchanges with the rest of society can be readily observed.

The Parsonian schema, as has already been emphasized, always points to two simultaneous modes of analysis. First the economy can be treated as a social system, differentiated from the other sub-systems of society and itself differentiated into sub-systems. This might be called vertical analysis, concerned with the economy on its own, its internal organization and functioning. The second approach consists of locating the economy within society and studying the interaction and interchanges between it and the other sub-systems of society. This is, so to speak, a horizontal analysis of the economy as one of the four sub-systems which together comprise society.[1]

4.1.1 *The Economic Sub-system*

The economy as understood by Parsons is neither a concrete structure nor an institution. Rather it is the aspect of people's activity relating to the production and distribution of goods and services necessary to the material survival and the well-being of individuals or collectivities. So the production and distribution of goods and services are what distinguish the economy. Any activity contributing to the production and distribution of goods and services falls within the economic network. At the same time, the production and distribution of goods and services define the boundaries of the economy. Once the goods and services have been produced and distributed, the way they are used, how they are consumed, why they are wanted and consumed are no concern of the economy. These are aspects of social activity which belong to other sub-systems of society.

Like any other system of action, the economy can be analysed in terms of the four-function paradigm; Parsons is able to distinguish four sub-systems within the economy and trace a network of exchanges between them. First, as has just been said, the economy is directed towards the goal of the production and distribution of goods and services. Its objective is to meet the needs of consumption by producing sufficient goods and services to meet the requirements of the members of a collectivity. So a sub-system can be identified within the economy, concerned with mobilizing resources to attain this objective; this corresponds to the *goal-attainment* (G) function in any system of action.

In pursuing this goal, the economic system must be able to draw on a reservoir of resources of different kinds. These may be material, like natural resources, but they are also, and perhaps more often, cultural and social psychological. Technology must be counted among necessary economic resources, and it is essentially something cultural. Similarly, the motivation of actors enters into productive roles and shapes them according to cultural norms and models; this is the problem of socializing actors to the exigencies of production and to the gratifications and sanctions it brings with it. Together, these physical, cultural and social psychological resources comprise what Parsons calls the *economic commitments* necessary for the economy to function effectively. They are the economy's *pattern-maintenance* (L) sub-system, which links it to both culture and personality.

Production also requires processes of capital formation. A proportion of consumption must be forgone in the short term in order that resources can be invested in productive capital—fixed plant and machinery, stocks of raw materials, labour training and so on—making possible increased production and therefore consumption in the long term. All activities which require *capitalization,* together with the specialized activities which spring up to meet this need, form the *adaptive* (A) sub-system of the economy. Its function is to select and procure the resources needed from the physical environment and the rest of the social system; it also costs up these resources and assesses what they are worth to the system.

Finally, co-ordination and organization of the factors of production are needed if the economy is to work effectively towards the attainment of productive goals. Here Parsons returns to the work of Marshall. To the classical trio of factors of production—labour, land and capital—Marshall added *organization,* the function of the entrepreneur and administrator. Parsons sees all *organizational activities* as the *integrative* (I) sub-system of the economy.

A   G

Capitalization and investment sub-system	Production sub-system—including distribution and sales
Economic commitments: Physical, cultural and motivational resources	Organizational sub-system: entrepreneurid function

L   I

(From *Economy and Society,* p 44)
Fig. 8 Functional Differentiation of Sub-systems of the Economy

It is not difficult to trace out a vast network of exchange and interaction between these four sub-systems of the economy. Thus investment serves to procure the various physical and social resources required for production. Similarly, the economy's integrative institutions have to be able to rely on their human resources; so in return for commitments, they pay monetary rewards and guarantee a certain security.

The laws of supply and demand are the most general principles governing all these exchanges; that is why they occupy such a central position in economic theory. Parsons stresses that they are only a special form of the more general principle of action and reaction found in every system of action. Demand can be seen as a kind of action in a market—either a factor market or product market—and the reaction to this action takes the form of supply. Or *vice versa*, supply can be seen as the action and demand as reaction. The supply and demand curves used by economists represent the most precise and refined use so far achieved of the principle of action and reaction. This is because in the economy the two fundamental elements in interaction—actions and sanctions—are both easily quantifiable, thanks to money being the common standard of measurement for economic activity. The value of goods or labour can be measured in terms of its cost, productivity and potential rent. And the actor supplying his labour can measure the gratifications or sanctions he receives in precise monetary terms. There is no other case in which the principle of action and reaction appears in such a clear and easily measured form.

For Parsons, the difference in 'visibility' between the laws of supply and demand and the principle of action and reaction is not fundamental. It is accidental, and does not alter the fact that supply and demand is a specific manifestation of the more general principle.

4.1.2 *Economy and Society*

Turning to the 'horizontal' mode of analysis, the economy can now be considered as a part of society. It is now taken not as a social system in itself, but as the adaptive sub-system of society. As such it enters into exchanges with the other sub-systems. Parsons sets out to trace these exchanges, and this makes his analysis dynamic. As Parsons describes it, the economy is not a static and equilibrated system but a very busy market, bound up with the even larger market of society through continual processes of exchange.

Figure 9,[2] which develops part of Fig. 6 in more detail, shows the network of exchanges between the economy and the other subsystems of society. In the four corners are shown the sub-systems of society—the economy, the polity, the societal community and the socialization system. Each of these sub-systems is subdivided in turn into four sub-systems. As the diagram shows, three of these internal sub-systems—the adaptive, goal-attainment and integrative ones—always act as intermediaries in the economy's exchanges with

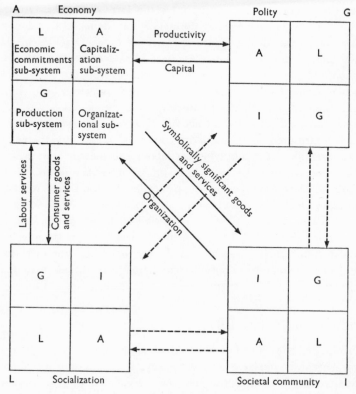

Fig. 9 Interchange Systems Between the Economy and other Sub-systems of Society

the other three sub-systems of society. Obviously it is the same for each of the other sub-systems in their relations with each other and with the economy. Parsons makes his systems of exchange rigorously symmetrical.

It should also be noted that though each of the four sub-systems of society contains its own pattern-maintenance (L) sub-system, this is not involved in the network of exchanges. The pattern-maintenance sub-sub-system is always a special case relative to the other three sub-sub-systems.

> To be sure, the latency sub-system of the society has boundary relations with the economy and the other two non-latent systems . . . But *its own* latency sub-system is not contiguous to any sub-system of any other primary system.[3]

The latency sub-sub-system is not involved in interaction in the same way as the other sub-sub-systems are. As Parsons and Smelser explain, its boundary 'is a cultural rather than an interaction boundary'. It draws in cultural rules, values and norms and psychological resources; it represents the *normative context* of social action but does not itself take part in action and interaction. But now let us look more closely at the interaction between the economy and the other three sub-systems which form its environment.

The socialization (L) sub-system contains the family and educational institutions. In relation to the economy, these institutions supply the various kinds of manpower and special skills required for the economy to pursue its goal of producing consumption goods and services. In exchange for manpower, the economy supplies the socialization institutions with the goods and services which they consume. It also supplies money and credit to help them buy the goods and services.

In its relations with the polity, the economy relies on the State and on those responsible for mobilizing and co-ordinating labour to act as guarantors of the capital required for production. According to Parsons, the base of the monetary and credit system is in the polity; political institutions possess the authority to control the volume of money and credit, and they can create, maintain or devalue the currency. So the economic system is based on political decisions. And political decisions are involved in making resources available for capital investment in the economy. In return for capital and credit, the economy supplies the polity with the economic output it requires.

Finally, the societal community sub-system supplies the economy with organization. Organization is what effects the *combination* of factors of production. This does not occur automatically. It is achieved broadly in two ways. Institutions, such as firms, factories and economic bureaucracies, maintain the flow of products representing old and well-established combinations of factors. The flow of *new* combinations of factors of production is, following Schumpeter, associated with the entrepreneurial function. What does the economy supply in return to the societal community? In considering this, it has to be realized that wealth and many goods and services have a variety of symbolic meanings throughout society. They serve to symbolize styles of life and define social classes. Even a donation to a political party or to charity represents the use of economic resources symbolically to express solidarity of one form or another. In short, the output of the economy to the societal community consists of products which have symbolic significance in non-economic contexts.[4]

Parsons emphasizes that money is the medium of exchange through which the economy makes its contribution to the other sub-systems. Households put their labour on the market in return for wages and salaries. A monetary rate of interest is paid to the polity for the finance received for capitalization. And the economy uses money to obtain the services of entrepreneurs and administrators. This gives a hint of Parsons's final borrowings from economic ideas. Economists have identified four factors of production : land, labour, capital and organization. To each of these 'real' factors there is a corresponding type of monetary income flow—rent, wages, interest and profit.

Counting factors of production as 'inputs' and production itself as 'outputs', Parsons is now able to draw up a table of what he calls double interchanges across the boundaries of each pair of sub-systems. Figure 10 summarizes the double interchanges between the economy and the other sub-systems, and shows the medium of exchange involved in each case. In each exchange there is an input of factors of production in both directions and an output of products in both directions.

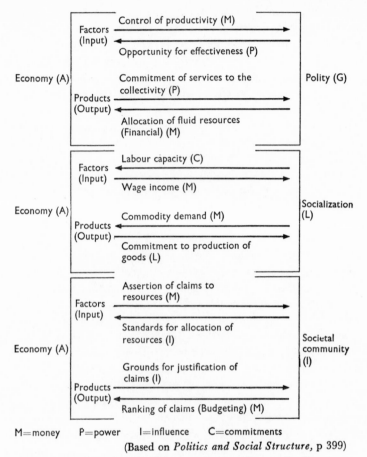

M=money   P=power   I=influence   C=commitments

(Based on *Politics and Social Structure,* p 399)

Fig. 10 The Network of Double Interchanges between the Economy
and other Sub-systems of Society

Parsons has taken a delight in complicating this table still further
by taking into account the hierarchical order of controls among
the media of exchange and within the interchange systems. These
refinements need not detain us.

4.1.3 *The Institutional Structure of the Economy*

It is important to bear in mind that Parsons's very narrow definition of sociology reduces it to the study of the integrative sub-
system in any system of action. In the case of a society, this means

that sociology mainly studies the societal community and its role in promoting solidarity. And in the economy considered as a social system, the same logic implies that economic sociology should study the economic institutions which integrate action within the economy. Parsons considers the most important economic institution to be *contract*; two others which stem from contract are *property* and *occupation*.

Contract is the most fundamental economic institution, for it institutionalizes and formalizes exchange between two or more parties very precisely. In contractual exchange, each party fills a role, makes some contribution, and expects some profit. Social rules and norms are embodied most explicitly in contract. Contract creates a real system of interaction and exchange between the parties to it. And this system can of course then be analysed into the four Parsonian sub-system categories. There are in fact four main elements in a contractual relation, each relating to one of the four sub-systems. First, there is a goal-attainment aspect : each party to the contract pursues an interest, each hoping to benefit by acquiring income, goods or services through the exchange. Second, the parties draw their motivation to enter into and respect the contract from a common universe of values. This is the pattern-maintenance aspect. Third, contractors have to accept some constraints on their freedom to enter into contracts, constraints imposed on them by their relations with the rest of society. Contracts must not only take account of the interests of the parties to the contract but also respect the interests of society in general and of other actors who may be affected by the contract. This is the imperative of adaptation. Fourth, over and above the exchange of money and goods and services, Parsons and Smelser claim there is usually a *secondary* performance–sanction exchange of a more symbolic kind. For example, proceeds from sales are not only essential to a firm's economic survival, they also symbolize its success and standing in public esteem. This is the integrative aspect in a contract, serving as institutionalized controls on the contracting parties.

Property and occupation are special cases of contract. *Property* is defined as the institutionalization of rights in non-social objects (or social objects in the case of slavery) which function as facilities in the process of production and as rewards to the factors of production. Ownership is seen as a contractual relation between a holder of property rights (a 'proprietor') and a productive unit, by which the proprietor's property is committed to productive functions. Parsons and Smelser therefore see ownership arising out of an explicit or implied *contract of investment*.[5]

Finally, the occupational sector of the economy centres on the institutions of the *labour market*. This is concerned with roles directly linked with production and distribution, be they independent roles like those of members of the liberal professions or of self-employed artisans like fishermen who own their own boats, or be they roles in great bureaucratic organizations. The labour market arises particularly from the *contract of employment* which may be either individual or collective, and very often remains implicit or only verbal.

In modern societies, progressive differentiation has taken place between the institutions of property and occupation. This differentiation has entailed the development of bureaucracies, which Parsons sees as a necessity in economic and industrial development. He maintains that family firms, large and small, played an essential part in the early stages of western industrialization. But the family firm combines three institutions in one : family and kinship, occupational roles and property. In the long run there is danger of this type of enterprise becoming an obstacle to the development of industrial society, which requires more universalistic forms of administration, possible only in a bureaucratic enterprise.

4.2 The Political System

Parsons has long believed that the theory of action allows him, or rather obliges him, to apply the same analytical scheme to each of the sub-systems of society. In particular, the mode of analysis applied to economics and economic sociology has been taken over lock, stock and barrel into political science and political sociology. Therein lies the originality and also one of the difficulties of Parsons's political analysis : it is intended to replicate his analysis of economic structures and processes as faithfully as possible.

From the beginning of his career Parsons was interested in political problems and in what he was later to call 'the political aspects of the social system'. His empirical essays prove this, as will be seen in chapter 6. However, it was at a later stage in his career that

Parsons really undertook an analysis of the political sub-system as a system of action.[6]

4.2.1 *The Political Sub-system*

Parsons's explicit intention was to demonstrate that political science is capable of attaining the same general theoretical level as economics. Hitherto, thanks to conditions favouring it, economics had been much more advanced than political science. Parsons became convinced that the time had come to lay the foundations of a political science equivalent to economics. In addition, he wanted to show that this political science had to be put together using components from the general theory of action and particularly from economics.

To fulfil these intentions, it was necessary to think of the polity as a sector of society or, in Parsonian terms, as a sub-system of society. That is why he uses the word 'polity' in a much wider sense than usual. For Parsons, the polity includes *all forms of decision-making and mobilization of human resources to achieve any objective defined (more or less explicitly) and pursued by a given collectivity.* The polity includes the definition of one or more collective goals, the mobilization of resources in the service of these goals, and the taking of decisions necessary for obtaining these goals. Now for Parsons, this political activity is not found only in the institutions of government, but also in every organization and association in society. Industrial and commercial enterprises, hospitals, universities, trade unions, political parties, social movements—all these involve a political function in Parsons's sense. The *polity* is not to be confused with *politics* in the narrow sense.

Parsons has not made an internal analysis of the political sub-system as he did of the economic sub-system. He has rather been interested in showing three things : that the idea of power can be treated as the equivalent in political science of money in economics; that the patterns of exchange and interaction between the political sub-system and the others can be depicted in the same way as the relations between the economy and the other sub-systems; and finally that political institutions are analogous to economic institutions.

Parsons baffled many political scientists by redefining power along the lines of money and making it a medium of exchange in the polity, and between the polity and the other sub-systems of society. Economics seemed to Parsons to have been created and developed around the idea of money, conceived both as a medium of exchange and as a symbol of the value of objects. In imitation, political science had to be formed around the analogous idea of power.

So Parsons introduced some original elements into his conception of power. First, power as defined by Parsons becomes something circulating in the interaction of actors and collectivities in all social systems. Power does not rest permanently in any one place. It is mobile and active, always leading to change and redistribution. A person in authority draws on a kind of reservoir of power which he exchanges in return for goods and services needed by the collectivity he controls.

Second, power necessarily takes on a symbolic character. Like money, power in itself is nothing. It is only valuable for what can be obtained in exchange for it. It also acts as a measure of authority; the further up the hierarchy a position of authority is, the larger the reservoir of power which it can deploy or put into circulation.

Third, there is not a fixed and unchanging quantity of power in society. The amount of power in circulation can increase and decrease, exactly like the volume of money. More power may come into circulation through a sort of 'credit multiplier'. This happens, for example, when a charismatic leader creates more power than has hitherto been in circulation in a society, on the credit of what he is able to do and people's faith in him. So there can be power inflation and deflation in the economic system, analogous to inflationary and deflationary movements in the economy. And counter-inflationary and counter-deflationary mechanisms can be observed in the political system just as in the economic system.

Fourth, Parsons links power to collective goals and to the idea of 'effectiveness'. The political system has to prove its effectiveness in achieving collective goals. Power is the instrument for achieving these goals, just as money is instrumental in the pursuit of economic well-being. The link between collective goals, effectiveness and power is, according to Parsons, parallel to the link between production, utility, and money in the economic system.

Fifth, Parsons makes a clear distinction between power and

authority. He defines authority as the code defining the use of power for members of a given collectivity. More concretely, this means that authority is :

> the aspect of a status in a system of social organization, namely its collective aspect, by virtue of which the incumbent is put in a position legitimately to make decisions that are binding, not only on himself but on the collectivity as a whole and hence on its member-units.[7]

This definition of authority is no more orthodox in political science than Parsons's definition of power. But it is consistent with the Parsonian notion of power, and the two complement each other; the notion of authority refers to a system within which power acquires its symbolic meaning for all members of a given society.

The five characteristics of power just listed enable Parsons to define it as follows :

> Power, then, is the generalized capacity to secure the perform-ance of binding obligations by units in a system of collective organization when the obligations are legitimized with reference to their bearing on collective goals and where in case of recalci-trance there is a presumption of enforcement by negative situa-tional sanctions—whatever the actual agency of that enforce-ment.[8]

From this definition it can be seen that power is ultimately based on physical force; in the last resort, power bestows on people in positions of authority the right to have recourse to force to make recalcitrants behave in the desired way. As a general rule, however, the right to use force is not immediately apparent in power. Power rather rests on secondary foundations which symbolize and take the place of force. So physical force is to power as gold and other precious metals are to money. Only during periods of severe crisis do people resort to using metals as money; in everyday trade, it is taken for granted that money is equivalent to metals. Similarly, it is only in periods of crisis that authority has recourse to physical force; in everyday life, it relies on other bases of legitimation.

In sum, power is the capacity to impose binding obligations on members of an organization to contribute to attaining the goals of that organization. Power includes the possibility of exercising coercion over others. But to Parsons it is essential not to confuse coercion with persuasion, for persuasion arises from influence, conceived as the medium of exchange associated with the societal community sub-system.[9]

4.2.2 *Polity and Society*

Defining power as a medium of exchange in constant circulation enabled Parsons to develop an analytical model of the political system in relation to the rest of society. Just like the economy, the polity in Parsons's conception is an autonomous and open system, across the boundaries of which exchanges are constantly taking place.

Figure 11[10] shows that the political system comprises four sub-systems, pattern-maintenance again being a special case not involved in the network of exchanges. The polity is involved in processes of exchange with the economic, societal community and socialization systems through its own adaptive, goal-attainment and integrative systems. Figure 12 depicts the systems of double interchanges of factors and products linking the political system to the other systems of society.

Between the polity and the economy, money is the principal means of exchange on the economic side and power on the political. Parsons calls this the 'resource mobilization system'. As far as factors are concerned, the economy brings to the polity what Parsons calls control of productivity—that is control over all productive resources necessary for the continued existence and prosperity of the collectivity which the polity maintains, mobilizes and directs. Understood in this sense, control of productivity becomes a 'factor of effectiveness' for the political system. In return, the polity supplies what Parsons calls 'opportunity for effectiveness', notably in the form of capital and credit put into circulation by the State for economic purposes.

In the exchange of products the economy commits services—typically employment—through the polity for the collectivity's purposes. In return, the polity allocates fluid resources—typically the control of budgeted funds—to the suppliers of these services, so that they can effectively fulfil their obligations.

In the exchange *between the polity and the societal community,* the media of exchange are influence and power rather than money

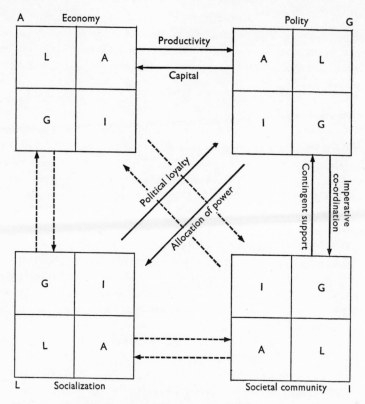

Fig. 11 Interchange Systems between the Polity and other Sub-
systems of Society

and power. In the exchange of factors, the polity supplies the
societal community with policy decisions. Policy decisions are a
'factor of solidarity' essential to the effective functioning of social
institutions. The social institutions in return feed into the polity
their demands, schemes and reactions. As Parsons explains,

> interest-demands 'definite the situation' for political decision-
> making—which of course is by no means to say that demands in
> their initial form are or should be simply 'granted' without
> modifications. Like other factors they are typically transformed
> in the course of the political process.[11]

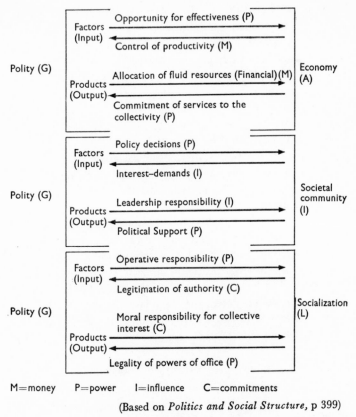

M=money   P=power   I=influence   C=commitments

(Based on *Politics and Social Structure,* p 399)

Fig. 12 The Network of Double Interchanges between the Polity and
the other Sub-systems of Society

As for products, the polity's output to the societal community
is 'leadership responsibility', which is necessary for the organization and activity of social institutions. And the institutions and
associations which form the societal community generate political
support for transmission to the polity. Parsons calls this double
interchange the political support system. What it really implies is
that a polity needs support in order to function, and the societal
community needs policy decisions in order to maintain solidarity,
and that therefore in any given collectivity there has to be some
kind of balance between authority and solidarity.

The third set of exchanges, *between the polity and pattern-maintenance,* involves commitments as a medium of exchange in place of money and influence. This is the 'legitimation system'. Again there is an exchange of factors. 'Operative responsibility' flows from the polity to the socialization sub-system; this means responsibility for the implementation and integrity of the system's value-principles. In return, the State derives legitimacy from the pattern-maintenance system. Max Weber's analysis of the different types of authority and their bases is, for example, relevant here. As for products, the polity grant to the pattern-maintenance system a sort of moral responsibility for the collective interests of the society in question, while in return the legal powers of the various positions of authority are defined.[12]

This, then, is the model which Parsons uses to throw light on the many links between the polity and the rest of society. The model may seem complicated, but it is in fact rather simplified as it rigorously follows the model already established for the economic system. Parsons set out to find the same type of exchange of factors and products across the boundaries of the polity as he had already found in the case of the economy. Some thoughts on this procedure will be given later.

4.2.3 *The Institutional Structure of the Polity*

When Parsons came to political sociology, he followed the same procedure : he drew an analogy with economic sociology. As he saw it, economic sociology should concentrate on studying three principal institutions in the economic system. In the political system, Parsons found three corresponding institutions—*leadership, authority* and *regulation*—the latter two being special cases of the first.

Leadership is the equivalent in the political system of contract in the economic system. It is the most diffuse, generalized and fundamental political institution.

By the institutionalization of leadership I mean the pattern of normative order by which certain sub-groups within a collectivity are, by virtue of the 'positions' they occupy within it, permitted and expected to take initiative and make decisions about attaining the goals of the collectivity, which bind the collectivity as a whole.[13]

Thus understood, the institution of leadership is found at various levels of social reality : at the level of a society in the form of the state; at the level of all kinds of bureaucratic organizations in the form of recognized positions of authority; and in movements and associations, where it is usual to speak of leadership in a more restricted sense. Whatever the level, leadership is an essential form of institutional organization. In some cases, it is both a concrete and a symbolic expression of a sense of solidarity, shared modes of thought, and feelings of community. In others, it is linked to the common interests and pursuit of common objectives for which the collectivity exists.

Authority is closely linked to leadership. We have already seen that Parsons distinguishes authority from power. Authority is the code defining the use of power, and power accumulates in and circulates among positions of authority. Parsons distinguishes three levels of authority. First there is authority which confers the power to take decisions binding on members of an organization. The second gives the power to distribute responsibilities among the members or units of an organization and to control the exercise of these responsibilities. The third kind of authority is over the allocation of disposable facilities, and control over finance, property and other resources.

These three types of authority fall into a cybernetic hierarchy. Anyone who has the authority to take decisions in the name of all members of the organization also has, *ipso facto*, authority over the allocation of responsibilities and facilities. This is the highest kind of authority because it exercises generalized control over the other levels of decision-making. The second level of authority, giving power to allocate responsibilities, necessarily carries with it the disposal of funds and resources required to carry out these responsibilities. The lowest kind of authority involves jurisdiction only over things, not over people and organizations. Parsons sees in this further proof of the extensive use that can be made of the principle of cybernetic hierarchy in sociology.

Regulation consists of the establishment of norms and rules which constitute the explicit framework of social control in any society. Law is the most obvious manifestation of this. But many other forms of regulation exist, especially in complex modern industrial societies. For example, every business firm has its own rules; the professions have long-established codes of ethics and sets of rules; the standards and procedures governing scientific research are another form of regulation, as is the discipline imposed on members of a party or social movement.

4.3 Conclusion

The principal criticism levelled at Parsons is that his sociology is static, that there is no place for change within it. In my opinion, there is scarcely any basis for this accusation. It should be clear by now that the Parsonian theory of social action hinges on the dynamics of interaction, networks of exchange, actions and reactions, disturbances and readjustments which are constantly involved in action.

The most serious theoretical difficulty really lies elsewhere. This chapter and the last have raised a crucial question about the whole of Parsonian theory : has Parsons succeeded in showing that the general scheme of analysis he has constructed is directly applicable to any and every system of action? More precisely, it has to be asked whether it is necessary for the general theory of action to involve the formulation of such symmetrical analytical schemes in every sphere of action.

It might well be asked whether Parsons has not, to some extent, deviated from Pareto's thought. Pareto put forward a sociology of which the central theme was to be the analysis of the social system, rather as economics studies the economic system. But Pareto was too conscious of the difference and even perhaps, in his view, the antithesis between the rationality economics attributes to economic behaviour and the non-rationality or irrationality of other social behaviour, to suggest that sociology use the same analytic model as economics. It would not be in the tradition of Pareto to imagine that the same analytic scheme could be applied to the study of residues and derivations as to rational behaviour.

In Parsons's defence, it must be said that he wished, with good reason, to discard Pareto's false dichotomy, and to classify behaviour and its motivation according to different typologies. But precisely because Parsons is very aware of the complexity of systems of action, especially social systems, and because he has shed more light than most sociologists on the multiplicity and complexity of systems, sub-systems and their ordering and arrangement, it is all the more surprising that he should want to bring all systems of action within the same explanatory scheme. To do this, he had to extend and generalize ideas developed in other disciplines, notably economics, in what sometimes seems an improper and certainly arbitrary way. The analogy which Parsons uses to transpose the ideas of factors of production, products, input–output and economic institutions into political science (and also psychology) ends up by imposing a rigid framework on reality. In the process, the danger is that reality is distorted and falsified.

However, this approach did enable Parsons to throw new light on certain aspects of social dynamics. In particular Parsons should be thanked for having developed the ideas of exchange between the sub-systems of society, of power and influence as media of exchange, and the analogy between an economic market and communication in the wider society. These are illuminating insights, though they have not yet fulfilled their promise.[14] The ideas underlying Parsons's original intentions remain rather interesting. Perhaps other sociologists will be able to return to them, and make Parsons's scheme more flexible and less slavishly tied to economic models.

NOTES

1. Parsons's most complete statement on economic theory and the sociology of the economy was written in collaboration with Neil Smelser— *Economy and Society: A Study in the Integration of Economic and Social Theory* (1956).
2. Fig. 9 is based on a diagram in *Economy and Society* (1956), p 68. We have tried to make it a little clearer by modifying both Rocher's and Parsons's and Smelser's versions. If it is still not exactly self-explanatory, we can only refer the reader to the discussion in *Economy and Society,* chapters 2 and 3. (SJM)
3. *Economy and Society,* p 69. We have slightly modified Rocher's exposition in this paragraph, drawing directly on Parsons and Smelser. (SJM)
4. Again, this paragraph represents a rather free synthesis of Rocher with Parsons and Smelser, *Economy and Society,* pp 65–6. (SJM)
5. In this paragraph we have again drawn directly on *Economy and Society,* in this case from p 123. (SJM)
6. Parsons has not produced one single book on political science equivalent to *Economy and Society* on economics and economic sociology. He has written on all kinds of political problems and aspects of political science, but in the form of articles widely scattered through books and journals. Fortunately, the principal articles by Parsons on politics have, thanks to

the initiative of W. C. Mitchell, been collected in one volume entitled *Politics and Social Structure* (New York, Free Press, 1969).

7. 'On the Concept of Political Power', in *Proceedings of the American Philosophical Society,* **107** 3, 1963, reprinted in *Politics and Social Structure,* p 372.

8. *Ibid,* p 361.

9. Rocher does not discuss 'influence' in detail. For Parsons's views, see 'On the Concept of Influence', *Public Opinion Quarterly* **27** 1, 1963, pp 37–62. The fourth and final medium of exchange is 'value-commitments', associated with the pattern-maintenance sub-system. On this, see 'On the Concept of Value-Commitments', *Sociological Inquiry* **38** 2, 1968, pp 135–60. These two articles are reprinted in *Politics and Social Structure,* chapters 15 and 16. (SJM)

10. Fig. 11, like Fig. 9, is based on *Economy and Society,* p 68, but we have tried to make it a little clearer than either Rocher's or Parsons's and Smelser's versions. (SJM)

11. *Politics and Social Structure,* p 401. We have inserted Parsons's own remark in place of Rocher's paraphrase here. (SJM)

12. By this point, Parsons's exchange imagery seems to me to be impossibly laboured. Readers may wish to compare this last paragraph with *Politics and Social Structure,* p 404. (SJM)

13. Talcott Parsons, *Structure and Process in Modern Societies* (1960), pp 149–50.

14. For a rather different estimate of the media of exchange in general and the analogy with communication in particular see J. S. Coleman, 'Comment on "On the Concept of Influence" ', *Public Opinion Quarterly* **27** 1, 1963, pp 63–82. (SJM)

5. The Structure and Development of Personality

It was predictable that Parsons should be led to undertake a psychological analysis of social action. There were several reasons for his turning in that direction. First, the idea of action, which is central to his whole theoretical apparatus, implied that the social actor possessed psychological energy and motivation which Parsons ought one day to attempt to explain. Second, in developing his general theory of action, Parsons came to accord an important place to the personality sub-system and its relations with the organism on the one hand and the social and cultural systems on the other. Third, Parsons took increasing interest in the work of Freud; Parsons said that he would have devoted an important part of his first book, *The Structure of Social Action,* to Freud had he become familiar with his work earlier.

Parsons's psychological theory sets out from Freud's. He has sought to extend and supplement Freudian theory, though criticizing it on some points. In reality, however, Parsons is not very Freudian, for his main objective has been to adapt the general theoretical model, already developed for all systems of action, to analysis of the personality. So Parsons approached the problem of the personality neither as a psychologist nor even as a sociologist, but as an action theorist. This is what makes him both an original and a rather isolated figure.

It is not surprising that Parsons's psychology is little known and rarely discussed. Few psychologists make much of it, because it is presented in a language which is rather strange to them; and few sociologists are interested in it, because they feel it is marginal to their interests.

As Parsons's psychological theory is intimately connected with the general theory of action and closely related to his sociology, its

99

broad outlines will be presented in this chapter. Inevitably many of the details and subtleties will have to be left out.[1]

5.1 Personality in the General System of Action

Parsons's first postulate is that the personality is a system of action and therefore can be analysed after the same fashion as any other system of action. More precisely, personality should be thought of as a sub-system of the general system of action, at once dependent on and independent of the other sub-systems. Parsons distinguishes personality from the other sub-systems, but sees it as functionally and dynamically linked to them.

This perspective gives Parsons a rather unusual conception of personality. *He defines the personality system as the area of relations between the organism and objects in the external environment, particularly social and cultural objects.* It takes the form of conduct or behaviour shaped by motives, attitudes and perceptions. More precisely, the basic organizational units of the process of behaviour are what Parsons calls *need-dispositions*. Need-dispositions are central to Parsons's conception of personality. Yet although he has used the term a great deal, it has remained ill-defined. Suffice it to say for the moment that need-dispositions are learned, not hereditary or instinctive. This distinguishes them from *drives*, which are biological in origin. Parsons also says that he uses two words— 'need' and 'disposition'—to make it clear that it simultaneously involves meeting some exigency of the personality system as well as a propensity to act or react in some way.

Parsons has added one other thing to his definition of personality. In the general system of action, personality is distinguished from other sub-systems by the primacy of goal-attainment. So personality is essentially teleological; need-dispositions define short-term and long-term objectives on which collective as well as individual behaviour hinges. This characteristic goal-attainment function of personality is predominant in relations between the personality and other sub-systems.

These relations are of a kind already familiar : relations of interdependence and exchange. A network of double interchanges establishes multiple links of interdependence between the personality and each of the three other sub-systems. Between the organism and the personality there are relationships analogous to those between the economy and the polity. The organism supplies the personality with the energy and adaptive capacities necessary for behaviour. The personality's particular role is to mobilize these resources and direct them towards the designated objectives. Thus, in Parsons's theory the personality system is closely related to its physiological and sensory-motor bases. It is through the organism's sensory apparatus that the personality is in contact with the external world, through the organism that it can manipulate physical objects, and from the organism that it draws its motivating energy. Parsons, however, insists that the personality is not just an extension of the organism; it is not merely behaviour under the control of drives and instincts. According to Parsons's cybernetic hierarchy, it is the personality which tends to exercise control over the organism; the control may vary in effectiveness, but it is always sought.

The exchange of sanctions and mutual support in interaction (the 'double contingency' situation mentioned above, pp 55–7) can be thought of as a system of exchange between personality and the social system. In effect, personality enters the social system in the form of social roles, for a role is really part of that aspect of personality called social identity. And roles define actors as social objects for each other. In any social relationship, the satisfactions that a subject seeks are conditioned on the one hand by the positive sanctions which other subjects can deploy and, on the other hand, by the satisfactions which other subjects themselves derive from the action of the first subject.[2]

In the exchange between personality and the cultural system, 'regulatory cues' fulfil the same function of control as do sanctions in the exchange between personality and the social system. From the point of view of personality, the principal function of culture is to supply norms and values which promote the internal psychological integration. Values and norms give the personality what Parsons calls its legitimation—the normative basis which stabilizes goals and orientates action.

One of the principal advantages Parsons sees in conceptualizing the relationship of personality to the organism, social system and culture in this way is that it avoids two extremes. It avoids falling into the biological reductionism which has dominated a good deal of psychological theory and used to attribute a predominant role to instincts or physiology. In Parsons's view, Freud did not avoid this error any more than the behaviourists. Parsons's own concept-ualization also avoids the opposite fault, associated with the 'culture and personality' school of anthropologists, who tended to empha-size the influence of culture on personality at the expense of biological factors. Parsons also criticized this school for not dis-tinguishing between the social and the cultural. Parsons's schema is intended to put the relationships between personality and the other sub-systems in a balanced perspective as well as to set out the hierarchy of controls and the direction in which they operate.

5.2 The Sub-systems of the Personality

When personality is taken as the system of reference, Parsonian theory requires that four sub-systems be identified within it, as in any system of action. However, Parsons has not made as thorough an analysis of the internal organization of the personality as he has of the social system, the economy and the general theory of action. Consequently the sub-systems of the personality are poorly defined and remain uncertain.

Parsons realized that Freud had already identified and analysed three sub-systems of the personality : the id, the ego, and the super-ego. But he has seemed to be in some doubt in using these three concepts, which do not fit very well into his four boxes. However, he considers that the personality is related to the organism mainly through the id, so the function of the id must be roughly that of adaptation. The ego mobilizes and directs the personality's resources in its internal and external relations, so it can be identified with goal-attainment. The function of the super-ego is to co-ordinate the id and ego, by means of internalized social roles and sanctions. This is where Parsons amends and supplements the Freudian scheme. The roles of the id and ego as defined by Freud seemed relatively clear to him, although in my opinion the meaning Parsons attributed to them differed from Freud's. But he paid most his attention to the super-ego because, since it seemed to be related to the functions both of integration and pattern-maintenance, he regarded it as ambiguous. To clarify the Freudian model, Parsons suggested that the super-ego fulfilled the same function as Freud himself originally assigned to it : the internalization of systems of interaction and significant social roles and sanctions. The super-ego therefore fulfils the integrative function within the personality; it is the means by which the norms and exigencies of the social system exercise control over the personality.

The picture still needed completing, however, with a fourth sub-system which Freud had not foreseen, corresponding to the function of pattern-maintenance, by which the personality relates to the cultural sphere of symbols, values, ideals and ideologies. Parsons now uses the term *identity* to designate the 'core system of meanings of an individual personality'[3] and this system fulfils the fourth function. Identity is learned in socialization, but once established it is the most stable component of personality :

> it cannot be changed by the more ordinary environmental re-wards and frustrations as mediated either through the ego or the id . . . It is more directly sensitive to super-ego influence but is still cybernetically superordinate to the super-ego.[4]

Identity in short, serves to co-ordinate the other sub-systems and their inter-relations, maintaining consistency, so that the individual acts 'in character'.

This analysis is, however, only sketched out in Parsons's work.[5] Generally speaking, Parsons has rather adhered to his own categories for analysing the organization and inter-relations of the sub-systems of the personality. So it is again the AGIL schema which prevails; Parsons feels more at ease with this than with any other analytical framework. However, he has used it in original ways particularly in developing a new classification of types of personality. This typology is based on the principle (mentioned above *à propos* Parsons's comparative sociology) that in any concrete system of action, the four sub-systems are not of equal importance. One or other of the sub-systems may attain primacy in a system of action because of particular circumstances, conditions or evolution. A system of action where adaptation is paramount will clearly have a quite different character from one in which goal-attainment, integration or pattern-maintenance is dominant. The distinctions can be pushed still further. Once the primacy of one of the four sub-systems has been established, the four resulting basic types can also vary according to the relative prominence of the other three sub-systems. Thus among systems of action in which adaptation has overall primacy, integration may yet be more important than pattern-maintenance, or *vice versa.*

The typology of personalities which Parsons constructs using this principle of relative prominence of the various sub-systems runs to as many as twenty-four different types, and we cannot explore all these possibilities in detail.[6] Instead the principal features of the four dominant types of personality described by Parsons will be sketched. Personalities in which goal-attainment is paramount are mainly orientated towards objectives external to themselves, directing their energy and resources to these ends. The result is that they are particularly interested in power. It will be recalled that power has a precise meaning in Parsons's political theory. Applied to the personality system it means the capacity to control the actions of others in the interest of goals pursued by ego. This kind of personality is prepared to forgo or defer immediate gratification when this is an obstacle to the pursuit of pre-determined goals.

The primacy of adaptation is associated with a generally utilitarian outlook and consequently with greater flexibility than the preceding case. This kind of personality will tend to gain more satisfaction than the first from immediate gratification. Immediate gratification in this context might be obtained from art for arts sake, knowledge for its intrinsic value or even wealth for the sheer pleasure of possession.

In these first two personality types, orientation is primarily towards external objects. In the other two, the internal organization of the personality system takes primacy. Where pattern-maintenance is predominant, the personality is organized around values or ideologies. This is the idealistic type of personality which tends to reject any compromise with practical necessities calling for various forms of adaptation.

The type of personality in which integration is predominant hinges on the internal equilibrium and harmony of the personality itself. Living in peace with oneself and others then becomes the over-riding objective, for which this kind of personality is prepared to sacrifice either other objectives or his personal values, according to whether pattern-maintenance or goal-attainment is the stronger subsidiary trait.

It can be seen that Parsons made use of his general analytical model to produce a classification which at least cannot be said to be devoid of interest. At any rate, this typology merits empirical verification by the development of personality tests along the lines it suggests.

5.3 Personality as a System of Action

The preceding served to locate the personality system within the framework of Parsons's general theory of action. It remains to analyse the internal organization and functioning of the personality.

It has already been remarked that Parsons thinks of the personality system as a system of action. That means that it possesses energy and integrative mechanisms which initiate and direct action. There are two facets to personality as a system of action—*performance* (or behaviour) and *learning*. These two aspects are complementary; any performance may involve learning, and learning necessarily takes place through a sequence of performances. But it is useful to distinguish these two facets of personality, regarding performance as the outcome of personality organization, and learning as the process by which the organization of the personality evolves. Though Parsons accords more prominence to learning, he has had to develop his analysis of behaviour or performances, and this will be discussed first.

Underlying all behaviour, Parsons posits the existence of need-dispositions, which are the essential driving force : they supply the motivation for action. As we have already noted, need-dispositions as Parsons defines them are not innate but learned. They develop progressively within the personality, proliferating through continual differentiation. In a young child, need-dispositions are not very numerous; they increase as the personality progresses towards maturity.

Need-dispositions can explain specific chains of conduct, because they establish actual causal links between particular goals, means and conditions. However, need-dispositions alone do not completely explain the organization of personality as a system of action. A second element is needed—values. Values make possible the links and connections between different need-dispositions necessary to maintain some kind of coherence in the arrangement of need-dispositions, and to give behaviour some long-term continuity.

This link between need-dispositions and values is concretely manifested in the establishment of social roles. The double contingency situation involving complementary role expectations in social interaction is important here. Through its performance of social roles, the personality organizes and arranges its need-dispositions so as to respond to the role-expectations and sanctions, and thus to establish some kind of correspondence between its need-dispositions and the values on which its roles are based. More generally it is through roles that generalized goals are ordered and specified in the course of interaction, and both values and need-dispositions are brought into agreement with these goals. This is the sense in which personality as a whole fulfils the goal-attainment function within the general theory of action.

In this perspective, personality clearly appears as the meeting-place of, on the one hand, motivation and energy, the roots of which are ultimately biological, and on the other hand, the values and norms of the socio-cultural environment. Personality occupies a rung in the middle of the cybernetic hierarchy: it is where energy 'from below' and information 'from above'—the conditioning factors imposed by the physical and biological environment and controlling factors originating in the socio-cultural sphere—come into contact and conflict with each other. This is why Parsons insists that the personality's goals are not imposed on it by single 'unit need-dispositions'; he rejects this as too psychologistic and ultimately biologistic. In order for behaviour to have coherence and consistency, the unit need-dispositions have to be arranged in a stable and orderly way. This can only be achieved through reference to values and goals which define and express role models and sanctions.

Personality organization requires one more thing. From outside itself, it needs supplies of two essential things, information and motivation. Parsons always uses the term information in a very general sense, to refer to any form of external signal received by the personality, the meaning of which it can decipher according to codes it has learnt. As for motivation, Parsons really means all the internal energy which could be described as fuel for the personality. This information and motivation can either be found in the environment external to the personality, or internalized within the personality. Parsons sees information and motivation as 'factors of action', and distinguishes between input factors and output factors. This distinction once more stems from the economic model which Parsons uses continually. And it is very important, for Parsons uses input–output balances in explaining psychopathology.

Figure 13[7] summarizes the main inputs and outputs of the personality system. Reading the motivation side of the table first, two kinds of rewards constitute principal ingredients of action for the

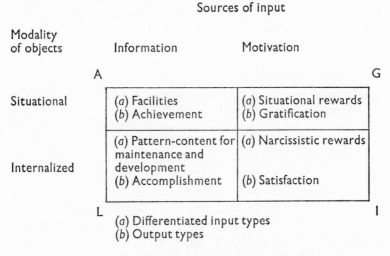

Fig. 13 Input–output Factors for the Personality System

personality. Situational rewards are the external objectives on which the personality determines in the expectation of one form of gratification or another. As for narcissistic rewards, these are objectives pursued by the personality in order to reduce internal tensions, in anticipation of various forms of satisfaction.

The information side of the table deals with the means necessary for obtaining rewards. Facilities or resources are used and manipulated in anticipation of achievements. And secondly the personality system needs an input of cultural models which contribute to its internal stability development and to successful accomplishment within a particular collectivity.

It can be seen that there is a regular relationship between inputs and outputs. There is also a complex network of relations between inputs; thus the rewards on which motivation is based are dependent on facilities and cultural models. Lastly, it should be noted that Parsons once more links the input–output complex to the four familiar AGIL categories.

5.4 The Psychology of Learning

As we have seen above, Parsons divides the subject-matter of psychology into two major categories, performance and learning. He considers learning far the more important for psychological theory —at least, he is much more interested in it. Learning is the crucial link between the personality and its socio-cultural environment; it accounts for the interpretation of the different sub-systems of action and frees psychology from biologism and instinctivism.

Like any other process, learning follows the Parsonian principle of differentiation and integration. It comes about by a process of differentiation successively dividing up structures into parts; in compensation, the process of integration establishes a new pattern of equilibrium and new functional relationships between the new units.

To this first principle Parsons adds a second, the principle of binary fission, which becomes very important in his psychological theory. Parsons maintains that differentiation in psychological systems always takes place by the division of existing units into two. For example, he applies this principle to the evolution of need-dispositions, using it to deduce what he calls a 'genealogy of need-dispositions'.[8] As will be shown in greater detail, the newborn child's personality possesses only one need-disposition, oral dependency. Following interaction with the mother, oral dependency subdivides at the time of the anal crisis into two need-dispositions, a need-disposition for dependency and one for autonomy. Then, in the next phase these two need-dispositions in turn subdivide into two more, and so on. Parsons believes this principle to be fundamental, and that it establishes that personality development is not the result of evolving instincts, but of a complex of processes explicable not in terms of biology but of the general theory of systems of action.

Aspects of meaning

Relation of objects	Cognitive aspect	Expressive aspect
A		G
Discrimination (Differentiation)	Cognitive discrimination	Relative deprivation (Selective reward and gratification)
Generalization (Integration)	Cognitive generalization	Generalization of cathexis
L		I

Fig. 14 Paradigm of Learning

Parsons also used the principle of differentiation to derive what he calls the paradigm of learning, set out in Fig. 14.[9] He says this is an adaptation of the input–output scheme shown in Fig. 13 to the process of learning. The two figures are based on the same distinctions : a distinction on the one hand between the cognitive and the expressive, corresponding to that between information and motivation; and a distinction on the other hand between discrimination and generalization, corresponding to that between the situational and the internalized.

This paradigm is intended to explain a complete cycle of learning in a given phase of socialization. Reading from A to L, all learning begins with a period of cognitive discrimination. This happens when behaviour, which in an earlier situation was successful, proves to be unsuccessful in a new situation, where it may positively impede goal-attainment and elicit punishment. 'Thus the infant must cry to get attention and food in the mother's absence, but in her presence, after a certain point in socialization, the same kind of crying will annoy her and cause her to withdraw rewards.'[10] The infant must be presented with clear and stable clues to enable it to discriminate between the two situations. It must be able to *compare* the gratification obtained from the same behaviour in one situation with the frustration it yields in another; this leads it to an experience of *relative deprivation*. The solution to the problem lies in seeking a new state of integration by means of cognitive and cathectic generalization. The new situation—the source of frustration—must come to arouse the same sentiments as objects already experienced as gratifying. This is achieved by symbolically associating the new situation with others which are already sources of satisfaction.

Parsons believes that this account of the learning sequence can be related to the mechanisms of socialization and personality pro-

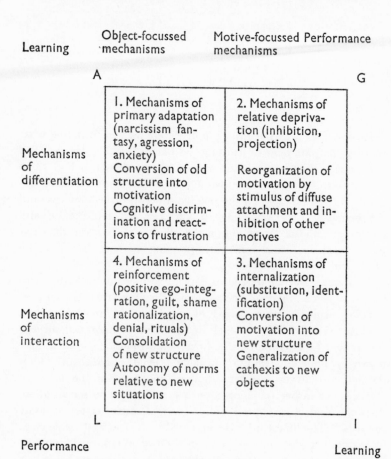

Learning	Object-focussed mechanisms	Motive-focussed Performance mechanisms
	A	G
Mechanisms of differentiation	1. Mechanisms of primary adaptation (narcissism fantasy, agression, anxiety) Conversion of old structure into motivation Cognitive discrimination and reactions to frustration	2. Mechanisms of relative deprivation (inhibition, projection) Reorganization of motivation by stimulus of diffuse attachment and inhibition of other motives
Mechanisms of interaction	4. Mechanisms of reinforcement (positive ego-integration, guilt, shame rationalization, denial, rituals) Consolidation of new structure Autonomy of norms relative to new situations	3. Mechanisms of internalization (substitution, identification) Conversion of motivation into new structure Generalization of cathexis to new objects
	L	I
Performance		Learning

Fig. 15 Classification of Personality and Socialization Mechanisms

cess identified and described by Freudian psycho-analysts. As Parsons interprets them, these mechanisms serve to maintain or re-establish equilibrium between inputs and outputs so as to regularize and harmonize psychological processes. The learning cycle necessarily involves disturbing the equilibrium between inputs and outputs as new information and motivation is introduced. So it is logical to attempt to complete the learning paradigm by bringing in the Freudian mechanisms. This is shown in Fig. 15.[11]

The four groups of mechanisms distinguished by Parsons each include a number of Freudian mechanisms. The mechanisms of primary adaptation include narcissistic gratification, fantasy, aggression and anxiety. Mechanisms of relative deprivation cover inhibition and projection. Substitution and identification fall into the category of mechanisms of internalization. And finally, the mechanisms of reinforcement include positive ego-integration and the super-ego mechanisms such as guilt, shame, rationalization or denial and tension-release through ritual.

5.5 The Phases of Socialization

Everything so far discussed in this chapter leads us finally to the phenomenon of the socialization of the personality which is of central interest to Parsons. This is the process which explains the genesis of need-dispositions, the sub-systems of the personality, and their organization and dynamics. From the beginning of human life and throughout its existence, personality, as defined by Parsons, has been formed and modified principally through its relations with given socio-cultural environments. Personality as a system of action develops relatively autonomously, according to its own needs and dynamics but using ingredients supplied by the other sub-systems of action, especially society and culture, but also the biological organism. Consequently, social and cultural systems are at least as important as, if not more important than, the biological organism in the development and structuring of personality.

Freud had caught a glimpse of this and shed some light on it. Parsons however added something new which Freud did not quite grasp. Personality as a system of action does not internalize social objects individually. What is assimilates are rather *systems of inter-action between social objects.* Parsons also changed Freud's emphasis in drawing attention to the structure of social relations which constitute the person's milieu at different stages in the life-cycle.

It was along these lines that Parsons attempted to make an original contribution to the analysis of socialization. He regarded the discovery of discontinuities in the socialization process as one of Freud's basic discoveries. But he considered that Freud had failed to make a systematic analysis of the structure of social relations as a system within which the process of socialization takes place. Parsons set out to rectify this omission. He works within the framework of Freud's account of the socialization process, but puts the emphasis on the systems of social relations which a person internalizes and which help to structure his psychological organization.

Parsons distinguishes four phases in personality development. These are set out in Fig. 16.[12] As Parsons stresses, the phases do not follow smoothly and continuously one after the other. Rather, socialization follows a discontinuous pattern; a person passes from

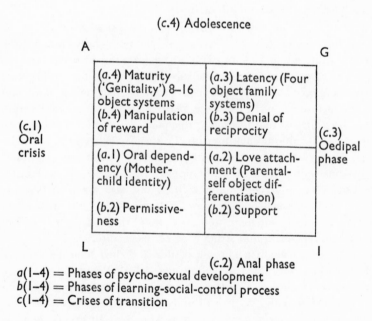

Fig. 16 The Four Phases of Socialization

a state of relative stability into one of crisis, the resolution of which leads into a new stage of stability at a higher level of organization and performance. The process unfolds 'in a spiral': socialization proceeds through a sequence of stages, each one more advanced than its predecessor.

Figure 16, which is to be read in the order L, I, G, A, summarizes this process. The stages marked (a.1) to (a.4) represent each of the four principal phases of relative stability in the personality system. Associated with each phase are particular mechanisms for learning social controls, and these are labelled (b.1) to (b.4). The breaks or crises, which disturb the periods of stability, precipitate change and result in a new stage in personality development, are labelled (c.1) to (c.4).

Parsons is especially interested in analysing the types of social relationship associated with each phase of development. The first phase, that of oral dependency, is associated with the simplest of all social relationships, that linking two people, the mother and child, the child being entirely dependent on the mother who gives it the basic gratifications it needs. Such social relationships form true social systems—the most elementary form of social system possible, as Parsons says. They are social systems because there are reciprocal expectations between the two actors, a simple pattern of communication based on an exchange of actions and reactions, and the rudiments of a code for interpreting these actions and interactions.

Parsons calls this the stage of oral dependency because the mouth plays the dominant role in the child's relationship with its mother. The transition of the foetus from 'pure organism' to infant is marked by what Parsons calls the 'oral crisis', involving the appearance of the need to receive nourishment through the mouth and also imposing the necessity of behavioural learning. Through feeding and the contact which accompanies it, the infant develops its first mode of interaction. The first mode of interaction is also the first mode of gratification, the mouth being the first means of gratification to develop in a definite way. Oral eroticism as a form of pleasure to which the personality will repeatedly resort originates in this stage.

The principal characteristic of this simple social system is that the mother (or mother substitute) is the source of all care for the child. That is why she becomes the object of its expectations and gratifications. The result is that the care given by the mother and expected by the child generates interaction between the two in which the child is very much the dependent party. The mother, as virtually the child's only means of satisfying its needs, has complete power over it, and the child is therefore in a state of almost total submission, anticipation and dependence.

The second phase is marked by the first differentiation between the mother and child. The child's identification with the mother is no longer so total as it was in the first phase. The infant begins to sense that his mother expects him 'to do something'. At the same time, what he is in fact able to do becomes more and more conditional upon his mother's approval and sanction. Thus the child becomes aware that he can, by his actions, manipulate his mother's approval and support.

What brings about the transition from the first to the second stage is the anal crisis. Freudian analysis showed that defecation is the young child's first personal production, and that he learns to make use of it in his relations with his parents, either to please or punish them. Defecation therefore assumes a deeply symbolic meaning in interaction. Because of this, Parsons sees the anal period as the occasion of the first binary fission : the child makes a distinction between itself and its mother or parents. The total identification with the mother is broken because the child can do something personal, and the relationship with the mother is partly conditioned by this.

In the second phase, the mother–child relationship is no longer one-way—the mother is no longer the sole contributor to the relationship. Consequently, reciprocity may be denied by one party or the other. The relationship becomes true interaction for both actors. That makes this phase particularly important in the socialization process, involving as it does the learning of a first social role and of the reciprocity of interaction between actors in complementary roles.

Another important aspect of this second phase of socialization is that the mother–child interaction is no longer dominated by care but increasingly by love. The child accords growing symbolic importance to maternal gestures and to the warmth and emotional security they express. The child, for his part, develops feelings of affection—the first truly social feelings he experiences.

Parsons believes that in the light of this analysis it is possible to reinterpret the primary narcissism discussed by Freud. He sees in it a misdirected form of identification with the mother. The child, 'instead of loving mother and looking to her reciprocal love, will tend to love only [its] own personality and look to internal sanctions of self-acceptance'.[13] So primary narcissism in the young child is a kind of mirror of maternal love which it can reproduce because it has completely understood and assimilated it in interaction with its mother.

The third phase is the one which Parsons considers the most important and deals with at greatest length. The point of transition to this stage is the Oedipal crisis, which Freud analysed so thoroughly. Parsons, however, reinterprets it in terms of family structure and social roles. When the Oedipal crisis occurs, the family comes to be perceived as differentiated into four social objects, distinguished from each other according to two principal criteria. The first is a hierarchical distinction between the parents of superior status and children of lower status; the second is the distinction of sex which cuts across the first. The differentiation between father and mother is more marked than in the preceding phases. And this difference relates not only to the sex of parents, but also the social meaning attached to one or other sex. In contemporary North American society, to which Parsons is referring, the father is the symbol of work, production and competition in the outside world; the mother remains the principal source of security, the symbol of love and unconditional acceptance.

This role differentiation exposes the child to universalistic and specific norms symbolized by the paternal role and particularistic and diffuse models associated with the maternal role. The breaking up of the parental role into two clearly distinct units is an important event in socialization, mainly because it is then that the child develops a more differentiated perception of social norms, and this contributes to the further differentiation of the internal structure of its personality. This process is completed by the child's progressive discovery of his own sex role. The little boy has to learn that there are behavioural norms which apply to him but not to a little girl, and *vice versa*. This is learnt through identification with the parent of the same sex, but also to a considerable extent by learning the role-expectations expressed by parents and other adults.

The learning of sex roles takes up an intensive period in the Oedipal phase; boys develop a particular attachment to their mother and girls to their father. The strongly erotic and affective character of the Oedipal period puts the child in a particularly strong emotional climate, favourable to identification with the parent of the same sex and, from the sociological point of view, to differentiation between the sex roles. Parsons here shed light on a social function of eroticism, which is to establish affective relations between parents and children suitable for learning the respective sex-role.

The Oedipal phase is not, however, experienced in the same way by boys and girls. According to Parsons, it subjects boys to more strain than it does girls. One reason for this is that girls can copy the maternal role more directly, whereas the most specific aspect of the paternal role—the occupational aspect—is external to the home. A boy does not have the concrete model of the masculine work role in front of him. On the other hand, he is in more frequent contact with his mother whereas a girl is in less frequent contact with her father. According to Parsons, this is why the Oedipus complex is stronger than the Electra complex and causes more serious disturbance.

This led Parsons to emphasize that the importance of the Oedipal phase of personality development, especially in boys, is closely associated with contemporary industrial society. The father's absence is more apparent in this type of society than any other, creating an asymmetry in the psychological development of boys and girls and stronger tensions in boys during the Oedipal phase than in girls. Parsons even went so far as to say that the notion of the Oedipal crisis in Freudian theory would probably be incomprehensible, even unthinkable, in any society other than modern industrial society.

In Freudian theory, the Oedipal phase is followed by a so-called latency period, in which the child's eroticism declines. In industrial society, this period coincides with the child's going to school, joining groups of children of the same age, and moving into a limited though nonetheless differentiated extra-familial world. The child now differentiates between the family in-group with which it hitherto identified, the first collectivity to which it belonged, and the world outside it—particularly the school. In the family, norms connected with the maternal figure are dominant; in the school setting the child comes into contact with the rules of the occupational and productive sphere. Differentiation between the paternal and maternal roles is completed by the differentiation between the family and other environments. Parsons counts the advent of education for all adolescents as a major historical event, because it resulted in greater differentiation in the general personality structure of the whole population of industrial societies. The educational system has in fact played a role of prime importance in the coming of industrial society, not only because it helps to train the manpower necessary for diverse occupational positions, but also—perhaps chiefly—because it has disseminated the universalistic, specific, activist and rationalistic norms which are the cultural basis of this kind of society.

Adolescence is another climacteric in personality development; it opens a new phase, leading up to the maturity of the personality—a practically limitless objective. Adolescence is marked by a state of tension between the various affective bonds created during the latency period between young people of the same sex—especially within peer-groups, cliques and gangs—and a return to Oedipal eroticism, manifested in a growing interest in the opposite sex. Here again, eroticism has an important social function—not the mere discovery of sex roles this time, but their progressive implementation.

A second feature of adolescence is the enlargement of the extra-familial world, the proliferation of new experiences in newly accessible contexts, and the gradual internalization of adult values. Psychological maturity is relative, however. Parsons argues that a personality with a more differentiated psychological structure will, if it is sufficiently well integrated, have greater maturity than a less differentiated personality. Consequently the extent to which social experiences in adolescence and post-adolescence offer a variety of new situations is critical in inducing greater differentiation of the personality.

In this perspective, Parsons sees an important difference in the socialization of those who proceed into higher education and those who do not. This finds expression in the differences between secondary school and university, and between the youth (or rather adolescent) culture and the student culture, which Parsons calls *studentry*.

Parsons was one of the first sociologists to emphasize, in the early 1950s, the importance of the youth sub-culture, both as a social phenomenon and as a phase in socialization. This sub-culture is linked both to the break that the adolescent has to make with his family, and to the pressures of the educational system. Adolescent culture, manifested in peer-groups, a communal style of life, and a certain marginality in relation to the wider society, accentuates the distance between the adolescent and his family environment. It denotes a sometimes brutal break with the restricted family circle and entry into the extra-familial world.

At the same time, adolescents undergoing the stresses and strains of the educational process find compensation in the milieu of the youth sub-culture. In contrast with the universalistic, specific and rationalistic pressures of education, the adolescent sub-culture puts the accent on *gemeinschaftlich* experiences characterized by particularism and diffuseness. Thus the youth culture prolongs certain traits of the family, but within a strongly egalitarian structure where disparities of age, experience and authority are abolished. In a society where the emphasis is on rationality and productivity, the adolescent culture represents both a sort of island of *Gemeinschaft* and an antechamber to adult life. The universalistic, specific, activist and rationalistic norms essential to industrial society provoke psychological tensions, perhaps particularly in the young; the youth sub-culture is one reaction to these tensions, a refuge from a certain harshness in the culture of industrial societies.

Since the Second World War, there has been a new educational revolution in the United States; not only does the majority of young people now finish high school, but nearly half of them enter university. Parsons thinks this prolongation of education for so large a proportion of young people is creating a fifth stage of socialization. Those who pursue their studies at university level, he says, develop a more differentiated personality structure than those who finish their studies after high school. University education involves more profound contact with what Parsons calls 'cognitive rationality', as a result of which the world is perceived according to more complex as well as more logical categories. But the university student has to endure prolonged submission to the authority of teachers, thus maintaining a situation rather like that in the family, at an age when a young person could lead a relatively autonomous and responsible existence. This prolonged state of inferiority and sub-mission is one of the sources of the discontent to which students are prone, and which is expressed in the search for new egalitarian forms of solidarity in protest movements and demands for the democratization of education. Unlike the adolescent sub-culture, the student sub-culture tends towards militancy and political action.

From another angle, a university career is an extended socialization for a particular occupational field, inculcating both specialized knowledge and a specific ethic. For the university student, socialization into the world of work is longer, deeper and more evident than for others. The significance of this statement will become more apparent later in relation to Parsons's discussion of the place of professionalization in industrial society.

5.6 The Pathology of the Personality

Parsons has carried his analysis of the personality over into the interpretation of pathological syndromes. To understand this we must return to Fig. 13 (on p 107). Psychopathological syndromes,

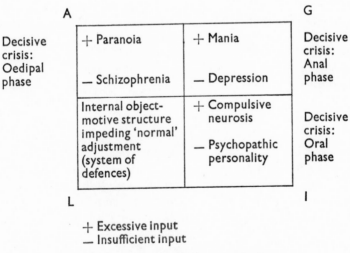

Fig. 17 The Principal Pathological Syndromes

according to Parsons, result from disequilibria between inputs and outputs—from the excess or deficiency of one or the other. In order to absorb a surplus or to compensate for a deficiency of inputs, the personality has to 'invest' excessively in certain defence mechanisms. Figure 17[14] sums up Parsons's thinking. It shows, for example, that paranoia results from an excessive input of information which inundates the personality and has to be rechannelled into the mechanism of projection. Schizophrenia, on the other hand, is characterized by a lack of communication with the outside world and a drying-up of information, the personality compensating by ever more exaggeratedly narcissistic solutions. Figure 17 also includes an element of aetiology; Parsons attempted to show the genetic link between these pathological syndromes and the first three phases of socialization.

5.7 Conclusion

Parsons has developed a very elaborate and detailed psychological theory. He might have been expected to put forward some very general ideas to enable him superficially to incorporate the main outlines of Freudian theory into his own scheme of analysis. But he has pushed his analysis of the personality system much further than that.

Parsons went so far, however, that it has to be asked to what extent he remained faithful to Freud, whom he claims as his inspiration. In the end, although it is couched in Freudian langauge, Parsons's psychological theory seems only faintly Freudian. In Freud's account instincts, drives and libido play a central part in the personality. The personality is organized around these—it channels, inhibits or suppresses them, makes use of them or resists them. Freud's originality was to demonstrate the dynamic importance of sexual and erotic instincts, even when they seem to have been suppressed. In contrast, in Parsonian theory, the personality is practically devoid of instincts; they are played down in favour of the internalization of cultural values and social norms. The id is no longer the bubbling cauldron of energy that it is in Freud. Certainly, the notion of need-disposition includes the idea of system requisites as well as that of inclinations and intentions. But Parsons insists that they are learned, not innate, which means they have

nothing in common with instincts. To avoid the biolological reductionism of instinct theories, Parsons has tended to present a strongly
'sociologized' picture of the personality. In the end, I believe Talcott Parsons's theory is closer to the American symbolic interactionist school, chiefly inspired by George Herbert Mead. It also
has affinities with American neo-Freudianism; such writers as
Erich Fromm, Erik Erikson and Karen Horney have also shown a
'sociologizing' tendency.

Furthermore, Parsons's description of the socialization process is
open to criticism. Since he dealt with this very much in the context of American society, it is curious that he should have used so
conservative a model of the American family. On this point, Parsons remains too orthodox a Freudian; it is not difficult to recognize in his description the bourgeois family familiar to Sigmund
Freud. Parsons takes no account of the profound changes which
have taken place in the American family or of their consequences
and potential consequences for the process of socialization. For
example, the fact that many women go out to work does not come
into the Parsonian model in any way; the same goes for separation
and divorce.[15] Why does Parsons not ask himself what consequences
a wife's going out to work is likely to have for the image of the
mother and her role in the socialization of children? Similarly, the
divorce and remarriage of husbands and wives profoundly change
relationships between parents and children.

Champions of 'Women's Liberation' have certainly not missed
the opportunity to attack Parsons for putting forward a traditional
image of women. He attributes an expressive role to them, strongly
flavoured with affectivity, particularism and diffuseness. This only
expresses the perception of women current in the American middle
class, thus giving credit to the inferior status against which American women are rebelling.

Finally, it is striking that socialization as Parsons describes it is
always a one-way process—the person being socialized is always a
child and it is always an adult who does the socializing. Yet in
times of rapid change, or in the case of immigrants, young people
can become the main socializing agents for their parents. Parsons
does not seem to have paid any attention to the socialization of
parents and adults in general by the young, a particularly notable
phenomenon in a society like the United States.

122   TALCOTT PARSONS AND AMERICAN SOCIOLOGY

NOTES

1. Parsons's psychology is to be found particularly in the following works:
Toward a General Theory of Action (1951), pp 110–58; *Family, Socialization and Interaction Process* (1955); *Social Structure and Personality*
(1969); 'An approach to Psychological Theory in Terms of a Theory of
Action', in *Psychology: A Study of a Science* edited by Sigmund Koch,
(New York, McGraw Hill, 1959) vol 3, pp 612–711; 'The Contribution
of Psycho-analysis to the Social Sciences', *Science and Psycho-analysis,*
4, 1961; 'The Position of Identity in the General Theory of Action', in
The Self in Social Interaction edited by C. Gordon and K. J. Gergen
(New York, John Wiley, 1968).
2. This paragraph is muddy in the French, and we have paraphrased as
best we can. The muddiness, of course, derives from Parsons's rigid
adherence to his model of interchanges between sub-systems. (SJM)
3. Talcott Parsons, 'The Position of Identity in the General Theory of
Action', in *The Self in Social Interaction* edited by C. Gordon and K. J.
Gergen (New York, John Wiley, 1968) p 14. (SJM)
4. *ibid*, p 20. We have inserted the two direct quotations from Parsons in
this paragraph in place of Rocher's paraphrase. (SJM)
5. 'The Position of Identity in the General Theory of Action', on which
this account is based, is Parsons's most recent statement on personality
theory. But there are differences between this article and what Parsons
wrote in *Family, Socialization and Interaction Process* in 1955. A rather
important development has taken place in his treatment of the id, ego
and super-ego, but it is not possible to deal with this here.
6. See 'An Approach to Psychological Theory in terms of the Theory of
Action', in *Psychology: A Study of a Science* edited by Sigmund Koch
(New York, McGraw Hill, 1959) vol 3, pp 659–71.
7. From *Family, Socialization and Interaction Process* (1955) p 176. The
terms achievement and accomplishment may seem near-synonyms, as
may gratification and satisfaction. Parsons explains the intended distinctions as follows: 'So far as the output of a personality system consists in
consummatory reward through relation to a situational object in a goal-
state we call it *gratification*. So far as it consists in narcissistic internal
reward derived from internal reward-relations between motivational sub-
systems we call it *satisfaction*. So far as it consists in maintenance or
improvement in situational object-relations in their instrumental significance as facilities, we call it *achievement*, and finally, so far as it consists in maintenance or improvement of the *internalized* object system
as value-patterns we call it *accomplishment*.' (*ibid* p 175). See also
Working Papers in the Theory of Action (1953) pp 215–19. (SJM)
8. See *Family, Socialization and Interaction Process*, p 149. (SJM)
9. From *ibid*, p 198. (SJM)
10. *ibid*, p 197. Rocher's exposition in this paragraph has been amplified
slightly by drawing on *ibid*, pp 193–9. (SJM)
11. From *ibid*, p 217. The more detailed classification is set out in *ibid*, pp
222–3. (SJM)
12. *ibid*, p 41.
13. *ibid*, p 73. (SJM)
14. *ibid*, p 254. (SJM)

15. Parsons does however discuss American divorce rates in *ibid,* pp 4–5, 24–5, and demonstrates his awareness of the effects of broken marriages on socialization in a footnote on pp 94–5. (SJM)

6. The Empirical Essays

There are many facets to Parsons's work and it is not always easy to reconcile all its aspects. In particular it includes a large number of sociological studies and essays of an empirical nature, which at first glance seem to have no connection with the wider theoretical enterprise, as if Parsons had from time to time simply abandoned his theories to consider major problems of the contemporary world or to analyse certain social phenomena which happened to interest him. Nothing could be further from the truth. The essays in empirical sociology are an integral part of Parsons's work; they are linked to the general theory of action as well as his general sociology. To neglect them is to acquire only an imperfect knowledge of the way Parsons works and how his theoretical system originated and developed.

What is more, these empirical essays conform with Parsons's conception of the sociologist's ethic. Parsons has often been accused of being an anchorite, on account of the high level of abstraction at which his thought is pitched and the difficult language he employs. Parsons has always believed and professed that it is the sociologist's duty to make clear to his contemporaries how their society functions and evolves, the choices open to them and the problems of conscience to which they must face up. Parsons does not, unlike Comte, think the sociologist should seek to exercise political power, but rather *influence*, which in his own sense of the term is something quite distinct from power. The sociologist's responsibility is to transmit the information he acquires to his fellow citizens as exactly and completely as possible, without misrepresentation, distortion or dissimulation. Such is the sociologist's specific contribution, *as a sociologist*, to social change and the solution of social problems. Parsons has been actively engaged in this task in his essays throughout his career. But, unlike C. Wright Mills or David Riesman, he has been badly served by his heavy, clumsy style and the complexity of his analytic procedure. Because of this, his essays have not become as widely known as he would no doubt have wished.

Parsons has grappled with a strikingly large number and variety of topics in his long series of essays. Few other American sociologists have shown such wide-ranging curiosity and a corresponding aptitude for dealing with the most diverse questions. Parsons's essays ramify in all directions, touching on almost every aspect of modern society. In fact, five of the dozen or so books which Parsons has published, either alone or in collaboration with other authors, are collections of previously published articles on similar themes. These are *Essays in Sociological Theory* (which has appeared in two editions in 1949 and 1954), *Structure and Process in Modern Societies* (1960), *Social Structure and Personality* (1964), *Sociological Theory and Modern Society* (1967) and *Politics and Social Structure* (1969). In addition, a considerable number of essays have not been included in these collections. So these studies amount to an important part of Parsons's work.

6.1. The Essays and the Theory

The empirical studies occupy an important position in relation to Parsons's more specifically theoretical work. In fact, few theorists have gone about their work as Parsons has. Theoreticians usually write large treatises expounding their theory as exhaustively as possible, not allowing themselves to be distracted by short-term works. Parsons, on the contrary, has written the greater part of his work in response to invitations to contribute articles, present papers, take part in seminars, conferences or discussions. Some of these articles and papers discuss pure theory alone. But mostly Parsons has dealt with the subjects suggested to him both from a theoretical and an empirical point of view.

Parsons saw in each of the invitations he accepted an opportunity to develop some aspect of his theoretical model or to confront it with new aspects of reality. The very general framework of the theory of action meant that Parsons recognized no limit to the new fields he could explore. Whatever the subject submitted to him, he could always—and theoretically he always had to—discover a systemic aspect of social action in it. His conceptual scheme implied that no question involving social action ought to fall outside its scope. So any empirical issue could be fitted into his theoretical system in one way or another.

A number of Parsons's major theoretical ideas developed out of empirical research and observation. For example, when at the outset of his career Parsons began to study the works of Marx, Sombart, Weber, Marshall, Pareto and Durkheim, he intended to compare their explanations of western capitalism and the development of modern industrial society. But from this research resulted Parsons's gradual discovery of what he interpreted to be the elements of a common theory in these authors, which he called the theory of action. This did not suddenly appear in Parsons's thought from nowhere; it germinated slowly out of the questions Parsons asked himself about contemporary western society.

Similarly, the pattern variables, which formed the kernel of Parsonian theory for several years, first arose out of Parsons's research into medical practice. From the very beginning of that study, Parsons ran up against the contrast which has often been drawn between the liberal professions and the world of industry and finance. The liberal professions, it is suggested, are characterized by a form of 'altruism'; they are vocations devoted to the pursuit of great objectives like health, justice or science. The industrial and financial world, on the other hand, has a reputation for self-interestedness, because profit maximization is its avowed goal and competition its dominant principle. Parsons thought there was some validity in this distinction and, as will be seen, made some use of it himself. But at the same time his investigations among doctors convinced him that the matter could not be left there. He had to break down this dichotomy in order to discern the characteristics of the whole occupational sphere, to which the liberal professions belong as much as do industry, finance and commerce.

In a first article published in 1939,[1] Parsons picked out three principal traits of the occupational sector of society: *rationality* as opposed to *traditionalism, functional specificity* as opposed to *diffuseness,* and *universalism* as opposed to *particularism.* He showed that these three traits—rationality, specificity and universalism—were common both to the liberal professions and to industry and commerce. The conjunction of these traits distinguished the occupational sphere from all other types of social institution. The first sketch of the pattern variables can be recognized here. Then in a subsequent article in 1942, where he dealt more specifically with medical practice, Parsons added another variable, *affective neutrality* as opposed to *affectivity*.[2] And Parsons came to realize that the pattern variables were useful for analysing not only occupational roles but also social stratification,[3] and family and kinship.[4] This led him to think that these were the basic structural dimensions of all social systems, and he made the pattern variables the main pivot of the theoretical model he set out in *The Social System* (1951). Finally, in *Toward a General Theory of Action,* which appeared the same year, Parsons went still further, showing that the pattern variables were the fundamental categories of any system of action.

This example of the evolution of Parsons's thinking clearly shows the close—and even causal—link between his empirical studies and the development of his theoretical model. At various times Parsons has returned to the pattern variables to refine them further, and has widened their scope first to all social systems and finally to systems of action in general. But it was empirical research—indeed his earliest empirical research, into the professions and especially medicine—which first prompted Parsons to think out the pattern variables.

Likewise, the four-function paradigm, another central element in Parsonian theory, grew out of empirical research on structure and process in small groups carried out by Robert Bales in his laboratory at Harvard. It will be recalled that in order to identify and classify the behaviour of participants in discussion groups, Bales had invented the idea of 'functional problems' which any group had continually to resolve in order to remain a functioning entity. Parsons saw these as the functional dimensions of all systems of action. The abundant and varied use he then made of them and the central position he gave them in his theoretical model must by now have become apparent.

Yet another case of the close relationship between theory and empirical research is Parsons's paradigm of deviance, to which we have not previously had occasion to refer.[5] Inspired this time by the work of Robert K. Merton,[6] Parsons set out particularly to show that each of Merton's types of deviance—exaggerated conformity and submissiveness ('ritualism') as much as innovation, retreatism and rebellion[7]—was related to different tensions in the social system. For this purpose, Parsons developed a paradigm of deviance based both on theoretical considerations and on a variety of empirical evidence. In particular, he drew on his own observations concerning family structure and relationships between its members, about illness as a form of deviance and relations between the sick person and those around him, and on Malinowski's observation of attitudes towards death.

If there are several forms of deviance there are in turn various modes of social control. Corresponding to the paradigm of deviance, there must therefore be a paradigm of mechanisms of social control. From the perspective of a given actor, deviance is either a non-response of other actors to his expectations or a response which frustrates his expectations. Mechanisms of social control are the means at the actor's disposal for developing and maintaining motivation on the part of other actors to fulfil his expectations. Now, as psycho-analysis has amply demonstrated, deviance results from states of tension which entail four principal types of reaction : anxiety, fantasy, hostility and defensive reactions. To counteract motivation towards deviance in others, the actor resorts—consciously or unconsciously—to suitable mechanisms for resolving these tensions.

The use of such mechanisms can be empirically observed in the methods used to teach children in the family and the school. They can also be seen in the activities of many kinds of social and political movements, as well as in judicial institutions. But the social relationship in which the mechanisms of control are most in evidence is that between a psychotherapist and his patient; in this case, recourse to mechanisms of control is conscious and systematically sought by the therapist. So they can best be identified in this sort of relationship.

Parsons here once more made use of what he observed during his study of doctors, who often have to play the part of psychotherapist; but above all he made use of the clinical experience he himself acquired through his own didactic analysis and instruction in psycho-analytic theory and practice. This led him to identify four mechanisms of control : first *support* intended to decrease anxiety and the need for reactions of hostility or defensiveness; second *permissiveness*, which allows the expression of strong emotions hitherto suppressed and unacknowledged; third, *denial of reciprocity*, which expresses the refusal to respond to hostility with hostility, anxiety with anxiety, so as to break the vicious circle of deviance; and fourth, the *manipulation of sanctions*, whether positive or negative.

These four mechanisms are used most explicitly and rationally by therapists in psychotherapeutic relationships. But all other forms of social control are based on the same mechanisms. For example, religious rites use them in a different but no less real way; as do judicial institutions and education in all its forms, whether in the family, in school, at work, or in social and political associations. Generally speaking, social control is weakened and disappears if these mechanisms cease to be effective or can no longer be employed, giving full vent to various forms of deviance.

These examples clearly illustrate the way in which Parsons made use of empirical observations from many different fields in creating components of his theoretical model, some of them quite central components. They demonstrate the close links between his empirical studies and his theoretical work.

6.2 The Diversity of the Empirical Studies

An adequate impression of the importance of the empirical studies in Parsons's sociology can, however, only be had from a complete survey of all the subjects he has touched on. His curiosity is seemingly unlimited, and has led him to consider a great variety of questions. Parsons's essays can be grouped into twelve themes, and it is useful to list and briefly review them.

1. The most general theme is certainly that of the characteristics of western industrial society. Strictly speaking, most of Parsons's essays and nearly all the following themes could be grouped under this rubric. From his first publications and throughout his work, Parsons has been busy describing, analysing, interpreting and explaining different aspects of modern industrial society. And for him this is embodied in its most advanced form in American society. So Parsons has written particularly about America, partly because he knows it best, but also because he considers it a sort of archetype of industrial society.

Some of Parsons's articles are specifically devoted to analysing the peculiar characteristics of industrial society. Two of these can be singled out; they complement each other and were written about the same time, a little before 1960. The first was a study of the 'institutional framework of economic development',[8] in which Parsons traced the evolution of the economic, bureaucratic and occupational structures of the western capitalist economy. From this, he tried to interpret the problem faced by present-day developing countries. The latter are evolving in very different context to that in which the Industrial Revolution took place in the west, so the institutional arrangements cannot be the same in the two cases. Parsons particularly insists that the role of the state in the developing countries must be much more important than it was in the history of western industrial development. In Europe and the United States, the lack of government intervention in economic matters—in accordance with the liberal doctrine of *laissez-faire*— allowed industrial, financial and commercial enterprise to develop more and more freely, breaking away from familial bonds and the vestiges of pre-industrial society. In contrast, in contemporary developing countries, it is the state which is best able to encourage universalistic behaviour and to be the principal agent of a new culture favourable to economic development.

In the first article, Parsons adopted an evolutionary and dynamic perspective. The second is more structural and deals with the principal characteristics of industrial society.[9] Parsons explicitly uses the idea of the four-functional sub-systems to describe the structural framework of the economy, polity, institutional system (societal community) and the motivation necessary to the functioning of an industrial society. In this article, the perspective is no longer developmental or diachronic, but very explicitly synchronic. It is difficult to say whether Parsons himself was fully aware of this difference but the complementarity of the two approaches in this pair of articles is quite striking.

2. A second theme runs through a long series of articles devoted to political issues, which have long attracted Parsons's attention. Parsons published his first political analyses during the Second World War. At that time he was deeply troubled by the rise of Nazism in Germany, a country in which he had studied and which he liked and respected. He wanted to know why Nazism had found fertile soil in German society.[10] More generally, he wanted to find

an explanation for the rise of fascist movements which several European countries had witnessed before the war.[11] At the end of the war, Parsons sought to explain the social and historical origins of Japanese militarism. His intention was to assess the chances of it declining after Japan's defeat, and what was required for it to do so.[12] A few years later, Parsons endeavoured to interpret the crisis American democracy underwent with McCarthyism. Many American academics were among the victims of that ideological luminary of the extreme Right. Parsons himself was actively engaged in the struggle against McCarthy at Harvard, and had to bear the consequences of it for some time. So he set out to explain this fascist upsurge and why it did not seem to him to have attracted such deep and lasting popular support as in Germany and Italy. Out of this came articles on the political effects of social strains in the United States,[13] the distribution of power in American society,[14] and the American democratic system.[15]

In these different analyses of political movements of the extreme Right, in Europe, Japan and America, Parsons's explanations were, in broad outline, almost identical. First he looked for structural changes capable of engendering particularly severe strains. In the cases he studied, these changes were generally consequences of economic development and industrialization : bureaucratization and professionalization of the labour force; extended education; techno-scientific rationality; changes in the occupational sphere and their consequences for the structure of family and kinship. The result was a generalized insecurity throughout society, often accompanied by a situation of anomie, to use Durkheim's term. This insecurity was felt most intensely in the higher social classes and ruling elites, which saw a threat to their interests, power and status. These are the classes and elites which have, as a rule, inspired, nurtured and supported ideologies of the extreme Right. Such ideologies have, however, found sympathetic echoes in the rest of the population, which has also been ready to listen to appeals to romanticism in an attempt to escape from the excessive rationalization of industrial society.

Lastly, Parsons has extended his analysis to the international plane. He has pointed the way towards systemic studies of international politics, in which the world scene is taken as the widest of all social systems and whole societies as the actors involved in interaction and exchange.[16]

3. Rationality has fostered such tensions in Europe and the United States because it occupies a dominant position in modern industrial society. It is embodied in many concrete forms of which one of the most important is bureaucratic organization. Following Max Weber, whose views on this subject he shares, Parsons sees bureaucracy as an essential feature of industrial society. It is a way of organizing work, made necessary by the growing multiplicity of tasks, by the ever more complex division of labour, and by the co-ordination consequently required for efficient production. For Parsons, bureaucracy is indispensable to industrial society, and it continues to spread and proliferate to encompass practically the whole occupational sphere.

As bureaucratic organization cannot be avoided, it is important to recognize it and understand it. So it is not surprising that Parsons wrote several articles analysing its various forms, its internal working, its interaction and exchange with the rest of the social system, and the psychological and social tensions it sets up.[17] And with that sense of continuity Parsons never fails to show, having studied medicine as one of the liberal professions, he analysed the mental hospital as an interesting case of bureaucratic organization.[18]

4. Parsons's interest in bureaucratization is accompanied by at least as great an interest in the position and function of the professions in modern industrial society. The part that Parsons's research into the medical profession played in the development of his theoretical model has already been mentioned. This research was his first empirical study, using interviews with doctors and participant observation; he obtained permission from several hospitals in the Boston area to don a white coat and make the rounds of the wards with groups of doctors. In view of this, it is easy to see why Parsons himself considered it 'a major failure of my career' that for various personal reasons he was unable to finish the detailed account of this research.[19] Parsons had in the end to content himself with a chapter about it in *The Social System* (chapter 10). However, he never stopped writing on the medical profession, approaching it from various angles : the doctor's relationships with his patients; the academic training of future doctors; the organization of the medical profession and its social and political conservatism; the image of the doctor in American society.[20]

In addition, partly inspired by his analysis of medical practice, Parsons has also analysed the legal profession and judicial institutions,[21] though rather more hastily and superficially. He particularly looked to see how the paradigm of social control could be applied to the activities of the legal profession.

These studies of medicine and law are not entirely explained by Parsons's theoretical interest in them. For a long time he has considered the growing professionalization of the occupational sphere and the dominant position of the professions to be among the most important characteristics of industrial society. For Parsons, a profession is any occupation needing a long preparation principally made up of theoretical or applied studies and practical experience such as clinical training in medicine, pupillage at the Bar and their equivalents. A profession is the application to useful ends of a particular sector of the cultural stock of knowledge; that is why the practice of a profession is usually subject to regulation by a guild or association. In pre-industrial society there were only a few recognizable professions : medicine, the law, and, after a fashion, the priesthood. Industrial society has witnessed a great proliferation of new professions and the professionalization of some former occupations : teachers, scientists and many other categories of intellectuals have now come to constitute professions in the true sense of the term. Because of the increasing necessity for scientific and technical work, and also the role of the mass media of communication, the structure of employment has changed, mainly through the appearance of what Parsons calls a vast 'professional complex'— the emergence of a great diversity of occupations of a professional character.

This phenomenon, which seems likely to continue, does not have only economic consequences; in Parsons's view it is of great historical importance. These professions provide new political as well as cultural leadership in the modern world. They have become a key element in the structure of modern society, for they take the place of the capitalist bourgeoisie. They play a dynamic role and fulfil the political functions of the ruling capitalist class of the nineteenth century. The same phenomenon can be observed as much in socialist as in capitalist societies as soon as they are sufficiently advanced; this seems to be what leads Parsons to think that the two kinds of society are converging to be more and more like each other.[22]

Parsons's conviction of the strategic role of the professions recently led him to embark on empirical research into American universities. As early as 1937, in a polemical article, Parsons raised his voice against those who wanted to create schools for professional training outside the universities; given the eminent position of the professions, he considered it in the interest both of the professions and the universities that the two remain closely associated.[23] After being interested for so long in adolescence and the economic and socializing functions of the secondary school, Parsons turned his attention to higher education which he believes is destined to have a dominant influence on the political, social and cultural outlook of contemporary society.[24]

Finally, Parsons has on several occasions discussed the 'moral' functions which he attributes to the professions. In a society dominated by competition and profit, they exhibit a degree of disinterestedness; they are the chief guardians of an important part of the cultural heritage; they constitute mechanisms of social control, through their role in socialization and the discipline they impose.

5. Associated with professionalization and bureaucratization in industrial society, and considerably reinforcing these two trends, has been a great expansion of the educational system. Education has at the same time come to fulfil more specific social functions. Parsons attaches great importance to the fact that the school in modern society has become progressively differentiated both from family environment, which in traditional society was the main institution of socialization, and from the Church, which was the first institution to take over from the family by developing a system of schools in most western countries. Schools have now become public institutions, directly or indirectly under the auspices of the State. Parsons lays emphasis on three specific social functions of the school. First it socializes new generations into the dominant values of society, especially those of the world beyond the family and most of all those of the occupational sector. So it is in school that the child learns to internalize the values of universalism, achievement, specificity and affective neutrality which it does not meet very much in the family circle, where other values are dominant. From this point of view, the socialization which takes place in the context

of the school is essential for the economic motivation, rationality and values typical of industrial society.

Second, the school acts as a channel through which human capital is allocated and distributed into the many and diverse occupations of modern society. From the secondary level onwards, the school serves to guide pupils towards jobs and professions according to their abilities, tastes and interests.[25]

Third, higher education is closely linked to scientific research and is a source of creativity, innovation and change. The university not only transmits knowledge but, perhaps more importantly, produces knowledge and subjects it to criticism, questioning and reinterpretation. As an academic deeply attached to universities as an institution, and conscious of the responsibilities of his position, Parsons has, as already remarked, devoted several studies to higher education. In one and the same institution, the university both carries out original research and trains people for the professions and higher administration. The university therefore fulfils vital functions in industrial society. This dual function in return creates a reservoir of influence (in Parsons's own precise meaning of the term) around and to the benefit of the university. Universities are able to draw on this influence to obtain the finances they need and the support of those in power.

6. Social stratification has been the subject of empirical as well as theoretical study on Parsons's part. The first article specifically concerned with this dates from 1940.[26] Inspired by Weber rather than Marx, Parsons established a clear distinction between social class and social stratification. For Parsons, social class is only one element in social stratification. Class is that hierarchical aspect of social stratification which is based on economic factors and family ties. More exactly, a social class is composed of numerous family units who have more or less the same standard of living, share a similar 'style of life' and have the same 'life chances' or absence of chances—such as opportunities for their children to be educated up to a certain standard.[27] Bonds of family and kinship enmesh people in social classes one way or another, for individuals may either be economically hampered by their kinship links or may obtain certain advantages from them. Social stratification, on the other hand, includes *all* forms of hierarchy resulting from the differ-

ential evaluation of individuals or groups on the basis of a variety of criteria. Criteria commonly used include family property, personal qualities, achievements, material possessions, power and authority.

In 1953, Parsons published a 'revised version' of his 1940 article.[28] By then he had put together the main components of his theoretical model which allowed him to make a more elaborate analysis of the place of social stratification in the social system. There is not space to go into this analysis in detail. Suffice it to say that Parsons tried to show that there was no such thing as a theory—a 'middle-range theory'—specifically of social stratification. Rather, as Parsons put it, the analysis of social stratification 'is general sociological theory pulled together with reference to a certain fundamental aspect of social systems'.[29]

The revised version of 1953 was, however, the outcome not only of Parsons's theoretical advances in the intervening years, but also of empirical research on aspirations and social mobility among high school boys in the Boston area which Parsons carried out over several years in collaboration with his colleagues Samuel Stouffer and Florence Kluckhohn and a team of students. Here again, the convergence of theoretical and empirical work in the development of Parsons's thought is very evident.

Unfortunately, the results of the study of social mobility among high school boys have not been published except in odds and ends.[30] Enough is known of these findings, however, for them to help to explain why, as soon as the post-war educational explosion began, Parsons was among the first American sociologists to claim that the main obstacle to access to secondary and higher education was not so much any shortage of economic resources as weak motivation. The factors favourable and unfavourable to academic and professional ambition would have to be sought out in the family, school and primary groups.

In an important article published in 1970,[31] Parsons undertook a second revision of his analysis of social class and social stratification. Recognizing that in his earlier essays he had been too exclusively interested in explaining only social inequality, Parsons adopted a new point of view. He put forward the thesis that modern society contains forces and factors which favour social equality as well as others which promote inequalities. These two groups of factors co-exist in complex societies and are part of their normal functioning.

So this type of society has to find various means of reconciling these contradictory forces and living with them.

Economic, technological and political developments over the last two centuries, as well as new social philosophies, have contributed to diminishing the power of four of the main historic forces for social inequality : religion, ethnicity, local and regional particularisms, and the division of society into classes or estates based on birth. New tendencies have emerged which favour equal rights of citizenship : the recognition of civil rights, democratization of political and educational institutions, the principle of equality of opportunity, and so on. But even the application of these principles creates new social inequalities. Equal opportunity for all has had the consequence of accentuating the importance of success (individual or collective) and of encouraging the emergence of inequalities no longer based on birth alone but also on talent and accomplishment. Similarly, political and social democratization has entailed a proliferation of bureaucratic organization and a high value being placed on technical and professional competence; these two processes in turn create inequalities different from those of non-industrial societies, but seemingly no less intractable.

Using his conceptual model, Parsons came to the conclusion that egalitarian tendencies are chiefly found in the integration and pattern-maintenance functions of the social system, the two functions that principally contribute to the internal organization of the system. The sources of inequality are mainly found in the functions regulating the social system's relationship with its external environment, adaptation (the economy) and goal-attainment (the polity).

Parsons rejects the idea that any total society can achieve absolute equality. Rather he postulates the necessary co-existence of pressures towards both equality and inequality. This assumption in turn raises two problems which every society has to resolve. The first is finding a satisfactory way to justify existing or newly created inequalities so that members of society will accept or at least tolerate them. The second is the problem of harmonizing leanings towards equality with actual inequalities. In response to these two problems, authoritarian régimes justify the concentration of authority and control in the hands of the political rulers in the name of values reckoned more important than individual liberty. This is the case with all one-party governments, be they socialist, fascist or religious. As against these absolutisms associated with strongly monolithic stratification, Parsons once more expresses his preference for a pluralist society of the liberal–democratic type. In the latter, there are many bases for the distribution of power and prestige, because it has a very complex pattern of stratification and social mobility.

7. Parsons has discussed the relationship of family and kinship to the characteristics of industrial society just outlined, especially in an American context. He developed the thesis that the extended family, characteristic of traditional and archaic societies, has had to undergo profound changes to adapt itself to the new requirements of the industrialization process. The geographical, occupational and social mobility required of the labour force undermines the type of family in which married brothers and sisters and their children live together with parents, grandparents, uncles, aunts and cousins. Members of the labour force need to be sufficiently independent to be able to change their employment, to move to new factories when they are established, and to move about within great bureaucratic organizations. The result is that in industrial society, the members of one family are not all on the same level of occupation, power, income or responsibility. The breaking up of the extended family in favour of the neo-local nuclear family, comprising only the father, mother and children, allows each member of a kinship network to follow his own career more freely, in accordance with his abilities, tastes and interests, and with the opportunities which present themselves. This development in family structure has gone hand in hand with the growing flexibility of social stratification, both of them facilitating social as well as occupational mobility.[32]

Following the same train of thought, Parsons turned his attention to social structures in American society linked to age and sex.[33] This essay dates from 1942, and Parsons was then one of the first American sociologists to see the youth culture as a characteristic phenomenon of contemporary industrial societies. Since then, of course, numerous studies have been made of this sub-culture, and it has become something of considerable importance, especially when it has spilt over into conflict and even violence. Parsons had great insight when, in 1942, he explained the youth sub-culture in terms of the strains and state of insecurity typically experienced by young people in industrial and especially American society. Parsons first became aware of youth movements and their social function in Germany. He was struck by the fact that the proliferation of youth movements and the rise of Nazism seemed to have the same roots : insecurity, the need for a sense of community, revolt against the past, a rejection of the present. Parsons then used these observations on German youth to explain the frustrations and strains which industrial society, by its very nature and needs, imposes on young people : prolonged study, individualism and competitiveness, the great value placed on productive activity, the bureaucratization of human relations, demythification, secularization and rationality. American youth, perhaps more than any other, was subjected to these pressures and showed signs of a malaise to which the youth culture is a partial response. Parsons sketched out his first analysis of this problem in 1942, and pursued it in much more detail in 1961,[34] just before the first tremors of the revolt which was to shake American youth for several years.

8. Another issue which Parsons could not ignore was whether modern society is inevitably an 'atomized' and culturally debased 'mass society'. He has discussed this question several times, and two aspects of it in particular : propaganda and mass communications.[35] Parsons does not think that these can be considered except in relation to other aspects of modern society. Indeed he has criticized those who think it possible to interpret modern society solely as a mass society[36] for having exaggerated the significance of just one aspect of it. Mass commuications can in fact be analysed in the same terms as other social structures. The mass media have grown to a seemingly dominant position by the same processes of structural change as Parsons has outlined elsewhere. Far from leading to cultural debasement, recent decades have seen the breaking down of ascriptive ties and a resulting *extension* of access to cultural opportunities to ever wider circles of the population. Second, the media and their content have become more *differentiated*. Third, Parsons argues that there has also been *upgrading* of cultural content—proportionately greater expansion of higher level culture than lower. And propaganda is not a new form of social control—its effects are simply magnified by techniques of mass communication.

9. If it seems a little odd to see propaganda and the mass media as potential agents of social integration, Parsons's insight that illness is a form of social deviance may seem even odder. This was the strange point of view which Parsons brought to his studies of attitudes to sickness and health, especially in advanced societies. After having analysed the medical profession and the hospital as a bureaucracy, Parsons rounded off his studies in this area by turning to the sick person himself and society's attitude towards him and his illness.[37] Parsons is unique in defining the invalid as a deviant, and he does so because a sick person cannot respond to normal expectations towards him, nor follow the rules of ordinary behaviour. A sick person makes the people around him behave in new ways towards him; his bodily needs entitle him to expect and even demand attention and moral support from those around him. Parsons found illness fascinating as a symbolic expression of social relationships, normal as well as deviant, between members of society. Similarly, he has studied attitudes towards old age and death in American society.[38] Malinowski had seen funeral rites as promoting social catharsis. In cases where the grief felt by survivors might take antisocial forms (suicide, depression, etc.), funeral rites serve as a recognized and valuable channel for the expression of anguish, sympathy and support by the social group. Parsons took up the main strands of Malinowski's thought, applying them to American society, and asking in particular how a social system which puts such value on activity and success is able at the same time to acknowledge the reality of ageing and death and to integrate these ideas into its culture.

10. The position and evolution of Christianity and religious institutions in the western world is another topic which has attracted Parsons's attention. The son of a Protestant minister, though an unbeliever himself, he has always approached religious questions respectfully. In his view, the sociologist should be fully conscious of the important psychological and social functions religion fulfils, mostly unrecognized, in the life of individuals and societies. The sociologist must realize that a scientific explanation of religious phenomena puts in question the strongest sense of purpose or meaning in life which a great many people have. Parsons seems to feel that it is almost impossible for religion not to exist, if not in its

original and traditional form, then at least in some indirect way. So he sometimes speaks of religion in a very broad sense, to include in particular Marxist–Leninist ideology—not its social scientific implications but its prophetic vision and ritualistic aspects.

Given the importance Parsons accords to religion, it is not surprising that he has devoted a good number of essays to it,[39] as well as taking it into account in many other studies, discussing religion from numerous and varied angles. For example, he has attempted to explain its origins by the frustrations and strains inherent in human life, especially life in society; he also sees religion as an important mechanism of integration, solidarity and social control, as well as causing differentiation through the divisions, conflicts and wars that it has brought about; inspired by Durkheim, he has drawn attention to the symbolic richness both of religious ideas and rituals; he has analysed the evolution of religious institutions, and their relationship to other institutions which command authority, power and wealth.

It is not possible to go into the details of all these essays. But one theme might be mentioned, because it marks Parsons's most recent thinking. He has tried to apply the principle of evolution to religion in two ways. First, he enthusiastically accepted Robert Bellah's thesis that the history of religions shows that they gradually become less tied to the social context of which they were initially a reflection and integral part, and become more and more spiritual, universal and personal.[40] Primitive religion was as much a form of social organization as a way of relating to the supernatural. Modern religion is more individualized, less and less institutional, and less closely tied to particular social groups. For Parsons, this thesis confirms that religious evolution takes place like social evolution, by the growing autonomy of the cultural sphere in relation to the social system, passing events, and the material conditions of life.

Second, Parsons has noted the differentiation which has taken place between religion or religious institutions and political power, law, the police and other social controls. The union of the sword and the cross seen in medieval Europe and many other societies was no doubt necessary in certain periods and civilizations. But it represents a primitive phase in comparison with the church–state division of modern nations. In the same way, canon law also served secular purposes for a time, but eventually gave rise to codes of civil law which have gradually grown away from canon law until they are totally independent of it. The church also had direct control over morals until this function was transferred to other institutions. Finally, a large part of the educational system originated within the church, before education became public and universal.

11. Several of Parsons's articles on religion might also fall into a second category, that of his essays on the sociology of knowledge. Parsons approached this vast area both theoretically and through various kinds of empirical analysis. From a theoretical point of view, he has tried to establish the boundaries of the sociology of knowledge,[41] which is not surprising in view of the importance which he gives to the distinction between culture and the social system. As for the empirical essays, the subject which, with religion, chiefly absorbed Parsons's attention was science, particularly social science. Throughout his life, he has been strongly and actively interested in the state and progress of the sciences and social sciences in the United States; he has often written on this. The sociological profession, its progress and position in American society clearly came to be one of his favourite topics.[42] But he was also concerned with the future of all the social sciences in America, realizing that practically and theoretically they were interdependent in their development.[43] On a broader front still, the study of American academic institutions which has been in progress for several years will perhaps constitute Parsons's main contribution to empirical research in the sociology of knowledge.

Finally, Parsons's numerous articles on the relations between the various social sciences might also be included here.[44] This is a subject which has occupied Parsons a great deal; it is a theme of strategic significance since the general theory of action was intended to be the conceptual and theoretical framework which united them all. But Parsons often discusses interdisciplinary relationships as much from the perspective of the sociology of knowledge as from a strictly logical point of view. This is what gives these articles an empirical twist, and allows them to be counted among Parsons's essays on the problems and progress of knowledge in modern societies.

12. Recently Parsons has turned towards another kind of problem that he had not previously confronted, that of ethnic minorities

in American society, especially the problem of the blacks. In collaboration with Kenneth Clark, he edited a collection of articles on the American negro, including an essay of his own earlier published in *Daedalus*.[45]

This essay does not really deal with the negro problem alone. Rather, it seeks to set it in the context of the history of ethnic minorities in the United States. Parsons developed the thesis that, contrary to the popular image of the American melting-pot, American society tended to absorb ethnic minorities not by a process of *assimilation* but by one of *inclusion*. The latter consisted of accepting ethnic minorities as they are, recognizing their existence as a fact, thus facilitating group mobility by which individuals benefited. German, Irish, Russian, Polish, Italian, French-Canadian and other minorities, each at first marginal to American society, have come one after the other to be accepted and recognized with their own customs, character and sometimes ethnic institutions such as churches, schools and social clubs.

Only the black minority has remained marginal. In this case, the process of inclusion has not worked, so that an important part of the American society has remained on the threshold of full and complete citizenship. But Parsons is confident that the same process which succeeded in integrating the other minority groups will work effectively once more in the case of the blacks.

It is not certain, however, that Parsons took sufficient account of the deep historic roots of the negro problem; he seems to have underestimated the growing obstacles to full integration of the black minority. He also seems to overlook other minorities in a similar predicament. These include the Chinese minority, trapped in the famous 'China-town' ghettos, and the Mexican-American minority who, particularly in California, form a rural proletariat on its great farms and in its canning factories.

These are the main directions in which Parsons has pushed his analysis of modern society. This outline of his essays and research gives some impression of Parsons's enormous academic output, his unquenchable curiosity, and the breadth of his interests and knowledge. It also helps to establish that, as has been emphasized, the main features of Parsonian theory originated in Parsons's accumulated observations of concrete reality or in problems he encountered in the course of empirical research. To those who criticize him for excessive abstractness, Parsons replies that there is what he calls a 'pragmatic' aspect to his work, meaning that his often erratic progress is explained by his way of producing articles in response to invitation and by the stress he has always placed on theorizing on the basis of concrete observation. Given his temperament, responding to invitations became a way of exploring new fields and meeting new intellectual challenges.

Reading his essays shows up another aspect of Parsons's approach which is often not recognized : his historical or diachronic perspective. Most of the essays deal with processes, evolution, the emergence of new phenomena, the adaptation of social structures to new situations, and with changes in functional systems. This is not surprising, for the industrialization of the western world and the transformation of political, economic and social structures have remained the central problem on which Parsons's thought has focused throughout his life and about which, in my opinion, his whole theoretical scheme is organized. Once again, I do not think that Parsonian sociology can justifiably be accused of being static. It is more historical and diachronic than most of his critics like to admit.

In my opinion, a more valid criticism is that Parsons has limited his field of study to capitalist industrial society, and almost exclusively to the United States. His occasional forays outside this field do not generally rest on very extensive documentation. In comparison with Max Weber, whose knowledge of history and other civilizations was vast, Parsons has scarcely stepped outside the narrow framework of the capitalist world of North America. For example, Parsons seems not to have taken any interest in comparative analysis of socialist and capitalist countries. They both appear much the same to him, in that they are both industrialized; only their political regimes distinguish them. This emphasis on industrialization as the essential phenomenon is linked with what in the next chapter we shall call Parsons's 'evolutionary functionalism'.

6.3 The Image of American Society

Precisely because Parsons takes the United States as his main and almost only field of observation, there is an image of American society underlying all his work, guiding it, and giving it coherence.

He has never made this image of American society entirely explicit, but it is possible to unravel its main features from the essays.

There is no doubt that the United States represents, for Parsons, the world's economically most advanced country because it is the most industrialized; and it is the most industrialized because of its Protestant origins, its democratic spirit and the development of its capitalist structure. Today's capitalism is not the same as that of the nineteenth century; it has evolved and adapted itself to new requirements, which it itself helped to create. In particular, American capitalism is no longer a capitalism of individual entrepreneurs and great family firms; it now consists mainly of vast managerial corporations, especially in the key sectors of industrial production. This is why Parsons sees bureaucratic organization, coupled with growing professionalization of the labour force, as the new and necessary form of production, not only in industry but also in commerce, finance and increasingly in the service sector—in hospitals and universities for example. The bureaucratic type of capitalism enables people with the necessary professional expertise to gain command of businesses. In the United States, capitalism evolved towards this new form sooner and more extensively than elsewhere. American economic activity therefore profited from a reservoir of talent that family businesses would not have been able to tap to the same extent. The evolution of American capitalism towards vast limited liability companies was as good as an infusion of new blood—the spirit of invention was renewed and a taste for risk and achievement regained.

However, though the American mentality accepted the bureaucratization of work fairly well and saw it as promoting economic progress, at the same time it remained suspicious of governmental bureaucracy. Americans continue to distrust the intervention of politicians and civil servants in their personal life and economic affairs. They have always retained a genuine, though perhaps naïve, faith in the virtues of private enterprise, liberty and individual initiative. These convictions are the basis of liberal democracy, as typified by the United States, in which much importance is placed on the ballot box as a counterbalance to the power of bureaucracy and public administration. In the context of liberal democracy, emphasis is often placed on the primacy of local as opposed to central power, so that municipal or State elections are frequently considered more important than national elections. Many questions are thought to be more effectively dealt with by local than central authorities, especially when the latter means bureaucrats, and many public undertakings are thought to benefit by being subject to local popular votes. This explains, for example, the large number of educational institutions, even in higher education, which are run by locally or regionally elected representatives.

One of the essential bases of liberal democracy is what Parsons calls pluralism, by which he means the official or quasi-official recognition of the diversity of interests which make up a modern society like the American nation. Conflict between pressure groups is an essential part of this type of society; it makes for cultural as well as economic wealth, dynamism and vitality. Here Parsons's analysis goes squarely against that of C. Wright Mills, who saw power in American society as concentrated in the hands of a small 'power elite'.[46] According to Parsons, Mills's picture is a simplification of a really much more complex situation. Mills saw a monolithic society where the plurality of interest groups, influence, power and authority needs to be emphasized instead. In pluralist liberal democracy, the loci of decision-making are numerous and widely distributed; pressure groups are allowed and even encouraged to proliferate. And the distrust of all centralization sometimes leads to excessive local autonomy at the expense of coherent planning and a unified political system.

Parsons also treats exaggerated descriptions of America as a mass society with some scepticism. Although he acknowledges that this view contains a grain of truth, it courts over-simplification, and tends to neglect the part played by the many associations, groups and clubs, which today, as in de Tocqueville's time, continue to be the most solid foundation of American democracy. Parsons interprets the multiplicity of churches and sects found in the United States in the same way. In short, the atomism of 'mass society' continues to be broken down by a great many voluntary associations with all kinds of objective. What Parsons calls 'institutional individualism', which remains for him the dominant trait of the American outlook and American society, should be interpreted in this sense. By this term he means the sort of social structure in which individual liberty is, as de Tocqueville observed, protected and guaranteed by the diversity and multiplicity of associations, and expressed within and through associations. A corollary is that these associations behave towards each other with the same kind of individualism as do their members.

One sphere in which pluralism and institutional individualism is particularly evident is that of ethnic minorities. Their inclusion into American society has not been achieved by forcing them all into one single mould, but rather by letting each define its own identity, retaining national customs and even a certain separateness. The 'melting-pot' seems to Parsons to be a myth.

In fact the hierarchy of ethnic and religious minorities is an important aspect of the pattern of stratification in American society. It is not a classless society, as for a long time many people liked to think. But the social classes are less rigid there than in some other societies, and longer-range social mobility is possible. This partly explains the mobility ethnic groups have experienced throughout American history : their members benefited by the social ascent of the whole group. But at the same time, ethnic minorities have been open groups for their members, permitting and even encouraging individual mobility. The educational system, both the public and private sectors of which are long established in the United States, was thus able to act as an important channel for social mobility independent of ethnic origins and religion.

In spite of this, Parsons does not see America as a harmonious society. There are, within it, notable sources of strains and friction. For a long time one of them has been the multiplicity of ethnic, religious and racial minorities in American life. The deepest are related to the high value placed on rationality, work, achievement and success, their concrete manifestions in economic activity, bureaucratic organization, science and technology, and the various reactions they call forth. These are harsh values, retaining the austerity of the puritanism and the commercial bourgeoisie from which they derive. Not surprisingly, there have been more or less overt forms of opposition to these values in American society—the youth sub-culture, political patronage,[47] and deviant and 'alternative' sub-cultures. Parsons fully endorses Max Weber's thesis on the role of puritanism in the development of capitalism, science and technology.[48] What is remarkable in the United States is that the puritan ethic has not remained confined to the Protestant population; it has spread to all ethnic and religious groups. This has made the United States a particularly competitive society, leading some to reject its consequences (youth sub-culture) and others to adopt crooked paths to success (political patronage, delinquency). Parsons also sees Protestantism as one of the sources of American pluralism, which involves the recognition and acceptance of the existence of differences and the conflicts which result from them.

The pluralist character of American society led Parsons to think that the strains within it will not cause abrupt or radical structural changes. Because pluralism allows and even encourages some sort of conflict between different interests, though considerable structural changes are at present afoot in American society, it is capable of carrying them out without radical rupture. Parsons does not envisage for example that the United States is likely to move from a capitalist mixed economy to radical socialism, or from a democratic to an authoritarian political regime. Rather, he reckons that the United States has the necessary resources and adaptability for evolution without revolution, and transformation without radical upsets.

What name can be put to the ideology which emerges from Parsons's image of American society? He can be described neither as a conservative nor a radical, but rather as a liberal imbued with the spirit of the Welfare State, the New Deal, and the mixed economy. He believes in the virtues neither of the *status quo* nor of revolution, but places his confidence in the structure dynamism of his society and in the progress of human rationality.

NOTES

1. 'The Professions and Social Structure', in *Essays in Sociological Theory* (revised edn, 1954), chapter 2, pp 34–49.
2. 'Propaganda and Social Control', *ibid*, chapter 8.
3. 'An Analytical Approach to the Theory of Social Stratification' (1940), *ibid*, chapter 4, at pp 78–9.
4. 'The Kinship System of the Contemporary United States' (1943), *ibid*, chapter 9, at pp 188–92.
5. This paradigm is presented most fully in *The Social System* (1951), chapter 7.
6. Robert K. Merton, *Social Theory and Social Structure*, enlarged edition, (New York, Free Press, 1968), chapters 6 and 7.
7. Parsons's categories differ slightly from Merton's, and Rocher here mixes the two sets of labels. For the sake of clarity, we thought it best to use Merton's more familiar terminology. Parsons explains the close relations between the two sets of categories in *The Social System*, pp 257–8. (SJM)

8. 'Some Reflections on the Institutional Framework of Economic Development' (1958), in *Structure and Process in Modern Societies,* chapter 3.
9. 'Some Principal Characteristics of Industrial Societies' (1961), *ibid,* chapter 4.
10. 'Democracy and Social Structure in Pre-Nazi Germany' (1942), in *Essays in Sociological Theory,* chapter 6, and in *Politics and Social Structure,* chapter 3. Also see 'Max Weber and the Contemporary Political Crisis' (1942), in *Politics and Social Structure,* chapter 5.
11. 'Some Sociological Aspects of the Fascist Movements' (1942), in *Essays in Sociological Theory,* chapter 7, and *Politics and Social Structure,* chapter 4.
12. 'Population and Social Structure of Japan' (1946), in *Essays in Sociological Theory,* chapter 13.
13. 'Social Strains in America' (1955), in *Politics and Social Structure,* chapter 7 (see also 'A Postscript—1962', pp 179–84). This article was first published under the title ' "McCarthyism" and American Social Tension : A Sociologist's View'.
14. 'The Distribution of Power in American Society' (1957), *ibid,* chapter 8.
15. '*Voting* and the Equilibrium of the American Political System' (1955), *ibid,* chapter 9.
16. 'Order and Community in the International Social System' (1961), *ibid,* chapter 12; 'Polarization of the World and the International Order' (1962), in *Sociological Theory and Modern Society,* chapter 14.
17. 'A Sociological Approach to the Theory of Organizations' (1955), in *Structure and Process in Modern Societies,* chapter 1; 'Some Ingredients of a General Theory of Formal Organization' (1958), *ibid,* chapter 2; 'Components and Types of Formal Organization', in *Comparative Administrative Theory* edited by P. P. Le Breton, (Seattle : University of Washington Press, 1968).
18. 'The Mental Hospital as a Type of Organization', in *The Patient and the Mental Hospital* edited by M. Greenblatt, D. J. Levinson and R. H. Williams, (New York: Free Press, 1957).
19. See Parsons's remarks on this research in 'On Building Social System Theory: A Personal History', *Daedalus* **99** 4, 1970, pp 834–40.
20. 'Illness and the Role of the Physician: A Sociological Perspective', *American Journal of Orthopsychiatry* **21**, 1951, pp 452–60; 'Some Trends of Change in American Society: Their Bearing on Medical Education' (1958), in *Structure and Process in Modern Societies,* chapter 9; 'Mental Illness and Spiritual Malaise: The Roles of the Psychiatrist and of the Minister of Religion' (1960), in *Social Structure and Personality,* chapter 11; 'Social Change and Medical Organization in the United States', *Annals of the American Academy of Political and Social Science,* **346**, 1963, pp 21–33; 'Some Theoretical Considerations Bearing on the Field of Medical Sociology' (1964), in *Social Structure and Personality,* chapter 12.
21. 'A Sociologist Looks at the Legal Profession' (1952), in *Essays in Sociological Theory,* chapter 18; 'The Law and Social Control', in *Law and Sociology* edited by W. M. Evan (New York, Free Press, 1962) pp 56–72.
22. See especially the article 'Professions', in the *International Encyclopaedia of the Social Sciences,* vol 12, pp 536–47; 'The Professions and Social Structure' (1939) in *Essays in Sociological Theory,* chapter 2; 'The

Intellectual: A Social Role Category', in *On Intellectuals* edited by P. Rieff (New York, Doubleday, 1964) pp 3–24; 'Research with Human Subjects and the Professional Complex', *Daedalus*, **98** 2, 1969, 325–61.

23. 'Remarks on Education and the Professions', *International Journal of Ethics*, **47** 3, 1937, 365–9.

24. 'Considerations on the American Academic System' (in collaboration with Gerald M. Platt), *Minerva* **6** 4, 1968, pp 497–523; *The American University* (with G. M. Platt and N. J. Smelser) (Cambridge, Mass., Harvard University Press, 1973).

25. 'The Social Environment of the Educational Process', in *Centennial*, Washington, D.C., American Association for the Advancement of Science, 1950, pp 36–40; 'The School Class as a Social System' (1959), in *Social Structure and Personality*, chapter 6.

26. 'An Analytical Approach to the Theory of Social Stratification' (1940), in *Essays in Sociological Theory*, chapter 4.

27. See 'Social Classes and Class Conflict in the Light of Recent Sociological Theory' (1949), *ibid*, chapter 15.

28. 'A Revised Analytical Approach to the Theory of Social Stratification', (1953), *ibid*, chapter 19.

29. *ibid*, p 439.

30. In the 1953 article, and also in *Working Papers in the Theory of Action*, p 254 ff.

31. 'Equality and Inequality in Modern Society, or Social Stratification Revisited', *Sociological Inquiry*, **40** 1, 1970, pp 13–72.

32. 'The Kinship System of the Contemporary United States' (1943), in *Essays in Sociological Theory*, chapter 9; 'The American Family: Its Relations to Personality and to the Social Structure', in *Family, Socialization and Interaction Process*, chapter 1.

33. 'Age and Sex in the Social Structure of the United States' (1942), in *Essays in Sociological Theory*, chapter 5.

34. 'Youth in the Context of American Society' (1961), in *Social Structure and Personality*, chapter 7.

35. 'Propaganda and Social Control' (1942), in *Essays in Sociological Theory*, chapter 8; 'The Mass Media and the Structure of American Society' (1960) (with Winston White), in *Politics and Social Structure*, chapter 10. (Rocher's exposition in this paragraph has been amplified by drawing on the latter article—SJM)

36. See for example *America as a Mass Society* edited by P. Olsen (New York, Free Press, 1963). (SJM)

37. 'Illness and the Role of the Physician: A Sociological Perspective', *op cit*, 'Illness, Therapy and the Modern Urban American Family' (in collaboration with Renée Fox), *Journal of Social Issues* **8** 1, 1953, pp 31–44; 'The Definitions of Health and Illness in the Light of American Values and Social Structure' (1958), in *Social Structure and Personality*, chapter 10.

38. 'The Ageing in American Society', *Law and Contemporary Problems*, 1962; 'Death in American Society' (co-author with Victor M. Lidz), in *Essays in Self-Destruction* edited by E. Schneidman (New York, Science House, 1967).

39. First of all, it will be recalled, Parsons translated Max Weber's *The Protestant Ethic and The Spirit of Capitalism* into English (1930). Among Parsons's essays on the sociology of religion may be mentioned:

'The Theoretical Development of the Sociology of Religion' (1944), in *Essays in Sociological Theory*, chapter 10; 'Religious Perspectives in College Teaching: Sociology and Social Psychology', in *Religious Perspectives in College Teaching* edited by H. N. Fairchild (New York, Ronald Press Co., 1952), pp 286–337; 'Some Comments on the Pattern of Religious Organization in the United States' (1958), in *Structure and Process in Modern Society*, chapter 10; 'Christianity and Modern Industrial Society' (1963), in *Sociological Theory and Modern Society*, chapter 12; 'The Nature of American Pluralism', in *Religion and Public Education* edited by T. Sizer (Boston, Houghton Mifflin, 1967), pp 249–61.

40. Robert N. Bellah, 'Religious Evolution', *American Sociological Review*, **29** 3, 1964, pp 358–74. (SJM)

41. 'The Role of Ideas in Social Action' (1938), in *Essays in Sociological Theory*, chapter 1; 'An Approach to the Sociology of Knowledge' (1959) in *Sociological Theory and Modern Society*, chapter 5.

42. 'Some Problems Confronting Sociology as a Profession', *American Sociological Review*, **24** 4, 1959, pp 547–59; 'Report of the Committee on the Profession' (a study group of the American Sociological Association chaired by Parsons), *ibid*, **25** 6, 1960, pp 945–6; 'The Sibley Report on Training in Sociology', *ibid*, **29** 5, 1964, pp 747–8; 'The Intellectual: A Social Role Category', in *On Intellectuals* edited by P. Rieff (New York, Doubleday, 1964) pp 3–24. Also see Parsons's editorials in *The American Sociologist*, during the two years (1966–7) he edited that journal.

43. 'The Science Legislation and the Role of the Social Sciences', *American Sociological Review*, **11** 6, 1946, pp 653–66; 'Graduate Training in Social Relations at Harvard', *Journal of General Education* **5**, 1951, pp 149–57.

44. 'Economics and Sociology: Marshall in Relation to the Thought of His Time', *Quarterly Journal of Economics* **46** 2, 1932, pp 316–47; 'Psychology and Sociology', in *For a Science of Social Man* edited by J. P. Gillen (New York, Macmillan, 1954), pp 67–102; 'The Concepts of Culture and of Social System' (with A. L. Kroeber), *American Sociological Review*, **23** 5, 1958, pp 582–3; 'Some Aspects of the Relation between Social Science and Ethics', in *The Sociology of Science* edited by B. Barber and W. Hirsch (New York, Free Press, 1962) pp 590–5; 'Unity and Diversity in the Modern Intellectual Disciplines: The Role of the Social Sciences' (1960), in *Sociological Theory and Modern Society*, chapter 6; 'Social Science and Theology', in *America and the Future of Theology* edited by W. A. Beardslee (Philadelphia, Westminster Press, 1967) pp 136–59; 'Law and Sociology: A Promising Courtship', in *The Path of Law from 1967*, edited by A. E. Sutherland (Cambridge, Mass., Harvard University Press, 1968); 'Theory in the Humanities and Sociology', *Daedalus* **99** 2, 1970, pp 495–523.

45. T. Parsons and K. Clark (eds), *The Negro American*, (Boston: Houghton Mifflin, 1966) which includes Parsons's essay 'Full Citizenship for the Negro American?', *Daedalus* **94** 4, 1965, pp 1009–54. (SJM)

46. C. Wright Mills, *The Power Elite* (New York, Oxford University Press, 1956). (SJM)

47. On the functions of the political machines and their patronage in American cities, see R. K. Merton, *op cit*, pp 126–36. (SJM)

48. On puritanism and science, see *ibid*, chapters 20 and 21. (SJM)

7. Parsonian Sociology: Influence and Controversy

Parsons's work spreads far beyond sociology. As we have seen, it covers a vast territory, since it represents a general theory of human action of which sociological theory proper is only one part. Parsons has, however, always described himself as a sociologist and continues to do so. In fact sociology is the central core about which the general theory of action is constructed. Parsons has had widespread influence and has provoked vigorous controversy in sociological circles. So, in assessing his achievement in this concluding chapter, his work must be set in the context of contemporary American sociology.

7.1. Talcott Parsons and Contemporary American Sociology

Parsons's place in pre-war American sociology was discussed in the first chapter. It was stressed that in the early stages of his career he played an innovative role, swimming against the current of American sociology as practised at that time. Subsequently, Parsons became progressively identified with American sociology, to the extent that critics sometimes failed to discriminate between the two. After having been criticized for not being sufficiently American, Parsons now has to take the blame for almost everything that American sociology is and does.

In one sense, this demonstrates the influence Parsons has exercised and continues to exercise. This influence is partly explained by the variety of topics he has dealt with in his articles and essays, almost always producing some new insight or an original synthesis. But the main reason is undoubtedly that amongst contemporary sociological theorists, both in America and throughout the world, Parsons has produced the broadest, most detailed and logically most integrated conceptual and analytical framework. Outside Parsonian theory, only Marxism offers the sociologist such an all-embracing theoretical system and tool of analysis. This unique position makes Parsons's work peculiarly important, but has also made it the target of numerous attacks. Parsons's influence has been felt not only by those who could be called his disciples and pupils and those who have derived ideas for research from him, but also by opponents of his thought, to the extent that they have had to take bearings from it.

To Parsons's credit, it has to be said that he was to a very considerable extent responsible for raising the level of discourse in American sociology. It is not necessary to agree with Parsons's theories to recognize that for more than forty years, with great tenacity and consistency, he has forced American sociology to face up to theoretical problems and to free itself from the empiricism in which it once seemed likely to become bogged down. Many of the lively debates which have taken place in American sociology in recent years have been due to a large extent to Parsons's direct or indirect influence. They include issues like the advantages and disadvantages of general theory, functionalism, scientific objectivity, Weberian sociology, the relationship between theory and empirical research, and the uses of cybernetics, information theory and exchange theory in sociology. Without the impact of Parsonian theory, American sociology would not have been the scene of intellectual excitement it has been.

Parsons did not enliven American sociology only on the theoretical plane. He also breathed new life into the sociological analysis of almost every aspect of social reality, injecting fresh insights and new hyotheses, suggesting new perspectives, and transforming traditional formulations of problems. There are very few fields of sociology where Parsons's influence cannot be traced, whether directly through his own writings or indirectly through his students, his followers and all those whose work has been influenced in various ways by him. Some fields show the effects of his own or his followers' influence more than others. This is particularly true of the sociology of knowledge and of science,[1] the sociology of religion,[2] economic sociology,[3] political sociology,[4] the sociology of education,[5] the sociology of social change,[6] and the history of social thought.[7]

Outside sociology, Parsons's work has met with little response in economics, anthropology or psychology in the United States.[8] Only in political science has his influence made itself felt. This is no doubt because political scientists feel more deficient from the conceptual and theoretical point of view than do economists or psychologists; Parsons's work offers them an analytical model directly applicable to their field. The political scientists most sensitive to Parsons's work belonged to the school of thought which set out to subject political structures and data to systemic analysis, putting the emphasis on communication and control. Notable among those influenced in varying degrees by Parsons are Karl Deutsch,[9] William Mitchell,[10] David Easton[11] and Amitai Etzioni.[12]

Finally, it is only superficially a paradox that Parsons's influence should extend to his most vigorous critics. It was largely in response to Parsonian sociology that what Americans call 'radical' sociology took shape. There is scarcely any Marxist sociology in the United States. 'Radical' sociology has taken its place. Though to some extent inspired by Marx, Lenin and other socialist thinkers, it really arose out of opposition to general sociological theory, to sociologists trying to keep their own personal values separate from their research findings, to objectivity in social science, to the use of notions like equilibrium, control, integration and function, and to the importance credited to values in sociological explanation. From this it is obvious why the chief exponents of this 'anti-establishment' sociology saw Parsons as the embodiment of all that they rejected. They set out to establish a 'new sociology' concentrating on the analysis of social conflicts, social problems, the concentration of power and subsequent oppression, class conflicts and social inequalities. Particularly forceful opposition to Parsons was expressed in the work of C. Wright Mills, who inspired and initiated this 'new sociology'.[13] It is also found in the writings of Horowitz[14] and Gouldner,[15] who are among Mills's best-known successors and who have for some years been the chief American critics of Parsonian sociology. It is significant that Gouldner devoted nearly half of *The Coming Crisis of Western Sociology* to a discussion of Parsons's thought. Conscious of the theoretical poverty of the 'new sociology', Gouldner saw a critical analysis of Parsons's work as the beginning of a regeneration of sociological thought. So American 'radical' sociology would not have been what it is, were it not for Parsons making it possible to be anti-Parsonian.

7.2 Functionalism in Parson's Theory

Parsons's interpreters and critics usually associate him with two contemporary schools of sociological thought : functionalism and value-consensus theory.

Parsons's theory is often thought of as the most perfect expression of functionalism, in the tradition of Spencer, Durkheim and Malinowski. This is because Parsons, in developing his framework of systemic analysis, made great use of the ideas of structure and function. It also stems from some by now rather outdated statements by Parsons on the usefulness of a functionalist approach in the social sciences. But it is a great oversimplification to see Parsons's sociology as the prototype of all functionalism, and equally so to reduce the whole of Parsonian theory to functionalism. In fact, functionalism has become a secondary aspect of Parsons's thought as his work has developed. And, in any case, there is not just one form of functionalism but many. Melford Spiro identified a dozen variants within American sociology alone.[16] Certainly, Malinowski's functionalism must not be confused with Merton's, nor Merton's with Parsons's.[17]

Three points can be made about Parsons's functionalism. First of all, it is a *systemic functionalism*. Unlike Malinowski and to some extent Merton, Parsons's type of functional analysis does not begin with particular social and cultural items and then proceed to explain their nature, existence and survival by their contribution to the organization and life of the whole. Rather he takes the whole as the point of departure, treating it as a system and analysing the conditions necessary for its survival, functioning, evolution and change. In this perspective, the term function refers to *various solutions to a particular complex of problems that a system can adopt in order to survive*, and 'survival' here includes persistence, evolution and transmutation. So for Parsons, functional analysis consists in establishing *a classification of the problems which every system must resolve* in order to exist and keep itself going.

Parsons derived this conception of functionalism from modern biology. He depends on biology for his claim that the idea of function is necessarily associated with that of living system, whether a biological system or a system of action. The idea of living system simply cannot be used without immediately coupling it with that of function. This leads to two modes of analysis. First, the system's component structures and the relationships between them can be identified; second, relationships between the system and its environment may be studied. Whether it focuses on the system's internal workings or on its relationship with its surroundings, Parsonian functional analysis aims to determine the *needs* of the system *as a system* and the means by which these needs may be satisfied.

This helps to make it clear what Parsons means when he says that the idea of function is related not to that of structure but rather to that of system. These twin ideas in turn point to another pair of ideas, structure and process. The idea of structure refers to the static and stabilized aspect of functions. That of process introduces the dynamic aspect, which for Parsons is as essential a corollary of the idea of function as that of structure.[18]

Second, Parsonian functionalism is concerned not only with systems *of* action but with systems *in* action. Contrary to popular belief, Parsons has long been preoccupied with the links between functional analysis and the study of change. Moreover, this explains why his thinking on functionalism has changed somewhat. There was a time when he thought that sociology, not having much in the way of genuine dynamic theory, ought to content itself with a second-best type of theory which he called 'structural-functional'. The failure of Pareto's attempt to develop a theory that was both systemic and dynamic seemed to Parsons to be an important lesson and an example to be avoided. In the absence of the flexibility and richness of dynamic theory, structural-functional theory seemed to Parsons to offer the advantage of a rigorous analytical framework, well-tried in the other sciences; the success of biology as the science concerned with organisms as living systems seemed to him to be particularly significant for the social sciences.[19]

Later on, Parsons discovered that he could make use of certain parts of cybernetics, information and exchange theory. These enabled him to give a dynamic twist to his model of systems of action and social systems, by bringing in the notions of interchange systems, media of exchange, input–output, and cybernetic hierarchy. As a result, he came to consider structural-functionalism as one stage in the development of theory in the social sciences. He believes that the model he has developed since 1953 has gone beyond that stage.

In the new model, the idea of function is dissociated from that of structure and linked instead to the concept of system, which puts it on the most general level of analysis where it belongs. Furthermore, in this new model, the idea of function serves to classify the activities of the system. These fall into two groups : processes of interaction and exchange between structures internal to the system, and between the system and others which comprise its environment. At both levels, as we have seen, functions are categorized according to the AGIL schema. Parsons believes that in this way his systemic model incorporates into functional analysis the dynamic, variable and changeable character of all systems of action.[20]

It is clear from this that Parsons, unlike many sociologists, does not see functionalism as a substantive social theory. His view is rather that scientific discourse always involves functional analysis in one form or another. He sees functional analysis as a sort of logic or language. More exactly, perhaps, he sees it as a set of languages which scientific reasoning employs in turn in order to move from one level of generality to a higher one, to reach ever more advanced degrees of precision and generality.

Thus in Parsons's conception, functional analysis is not something inherently static. Nor does it take just one single form. As a science develops through various stages, the kind of functional analysis it employs may undergo several reformulations. Few sociologists have created such a flexible, dynamic and exacting conception of functionalism.

The third characteristic of Parsonian functionalism, however, in my view detracts from its merits. It is an *evolutionary functionalism*. For a long time Parsons resisted evolutionism but, as we have already seen, eventually came round to adopting it. But unbeknown to himself, Parsons really always was an evolutionist and his functionalism was strongly coloured by this. For example, he always considered modern industrial society to be the most complete and finished form of social system because it has the greatest degree of functional differentiation. For theorists in the social sciences, industrial society provides the best field for observation, since the functions which are still fused together in less advanced societies are each clearly discernible in industrial societies. Pre-industrial societies are useful for purposes of comparison, but industrial society is the sociologists' chief laboratory, as they have felt instinctively for a long time.

Thus, from the beginning of his career, well before he explicitly took up an evolutionist stance, Parsons shared the nineteenth-century evolutionists' postulate that industrial society is the most advanced form of society because it is the most complex. To Parsons too, industrial society is the end of a long road, the culmination of a slow process of maturation. It is the most finished form of society because social organization and human rationality find their finest expression within it.

From this, I think, stems the static approach of which Parsons is often accused, rather than from his functionalism as is erroneously alleged. In fact Parsonian functionalism in itself is a dynamic approach. But it is thwarted by the evolutionist interpretation of industrial society as the final peak reached after a long and difficult climb. Underlying the accidents of history Parsons, very much like Comte and Spencer, sees a basic trend from primitive, undifferentiated societies, through archaic and intermediate societies to modern industrial society. This is the final outcome of long ripening and maturation. Parsons cannot—or does not want to—envisage this kind of society giving way to another without a regression to an earlier stage of development. Certainly he believes that industrial society needs to be perfected in many ways, but only by developing further along its present lines, not by radical changes. That explains why Parsons has not concerned himself very much with the possible features of post-industrial society, which a good many other sociologists are already examining and speculating about—a civilization of leisure, permanent education and new forms of mass communication, seeking new ways of perceiving reality and new patterns of social life.

Evolutionary functionalism, as we have remarked before, also prevented Parsons from taking an interest in the comparative analysis of capitalist and socialist societies, and in the contribution such studies can make to historical knowledge. As a result, Parsons has effectively studied only capitalist society.

Parsons's functionalism has been much criticized. Many sociologists have made it their principal target. However, in my view, the limitations of Parsonian sociology stem more from his latent evolutionism than his functionalism, and it calls for more reservations. Nor is it at all certain that Parsons's supposed social conservatism can be attributed to his functionalism. Alvin Gouldner came to the conclusion that sociological functionalism carries with it an inherently conservative view of society.[21] But his argument is not very convincing. It could equally well be argued that functionalism can as easily be combined with progressivism or even radicalism as with conservatism, just as the study of social conflict can go hand in hand with a static view of society, as Lewis Coser's work demonstrates.[22] If today Parsons seems a conservative figure in relation to critical, radical or Marxist sociology, there was a time when he was more liberal and progressive than the majority of his American colleagues—and that was precisely when he was at his most functionalist.

7.3 Talcott Parsons's Sociology of Values

Identifying Parsons with the sociology of values is no less a source of confusion than identifying him with functionalism. It is often said that Parsonian sociology elevates values to a determining role in social life and social organization. Contrasts are drawn between Marxist theory and what is taken to be Parsons's subjectivist idealism, or between conflict theories and Parsons's consensus theory. This deserves closer scrutiny.

First, what of Parsons's alleged subjectivism? In his analysis of social action, Parsons emphasized the symbolic nature—the meaningfulness—of human action, contrary to behaviourist and positivist theories. For Parsons, objects with which the human actor is in contract or interaction are always perceived and interpreted through a symbolic universe which gives them meaning. Man does not relate directly and immediately to the people and objects around him, nor even to himself; all relationships with other objects and with his own self are symbolically mediated. In Parsons's view, people and objects can have no direct influence on the social actor; the actor always reinterprets things and invests them with meaning. This is precisely how human action differs from the social behaviour of other animals. The sphere of values and beliefs represents a great break in the chain of evolution between *homo sapiens* and other species of animals. This is why the cultural sub-system of values, symbols and knowledge is so important : it is the source of all meaning for every social actor.

Parsons came to insist on the collective nature of the stock of symbols and values to such an extent that he practically drained the personality of any real subjectivity. As I argued in chapter 5, instincts and drives disappear from the personality system as Parsons describes it, only to make way for two subjective elements : need-dispositions, which are learned and result from the internalization of norms, roles, values and knowledge; and the function of goal specification (G) which in the end is perhaps the kernel of the personality. Need-dispositions are essentially the socio-cultural environment internalized, so the definition of goals is the only subjective component left inside the actor, and it is difficult to say precisely how far even that is individual rather than social. The personality is almost entirely absorbed by the social. It is true that Parsons takes the subject's point of view, not social structure, as the starting point of his theory. But the subject is defined very much as a social actor, in whom the springs of action mainly originate in the internalization of the socio-cultural environment. If Parsons is a reductionist, he is not a psychological but a sociological reductionist. This probably explains why psychologists have not felt there to be much of value to them in Parsonian theory.

As for idealism in Parsons's theory, it is expressed chiefly in the cybernetic hierarchy which, as Parsons uses it, seems to imply that values alone finally determine all action. Parsons can be rightly criticized for drawing oversimplified conclusions from his own model; it involves both energy and information, and he tends to pay little more than lip service to the interaction of the two. The cybernetic hierarchy implies that *action is the joint outcome of conditioning factors and controlling factors.* By 'conditioning factors' is meant the motivation for and constraints upon action deriving from the energy which arises in what may be called the infrastructure of every system of action. 'Controlling factors' signify the influence of information originating in the ideological superstructure—the organization and general orientation of action in the system. This concurrence of the two kinds of factors is essential to any system of a cybernetic kind, and therefore to any system of action. There is a continuous coming and going between the superstructure and infrastructure as energy and information are exchanged between the components parts of the cybernetic system.

But this is precisely what is not apparent in the Parsonian system of action. Horrified by the behaviourism prevalent in the social sciences at the beginning of his career, Parsons saw the need to stress the role of internalized values in human action. This led him somewhat to distort his own model, using it in a rather garbled way with too much emphasis put on the role of factors of control and leaving the conditioning factors out in the cold. He thereby laid himself open to the charge of exaggerating the dominance of values at the expense of other factors—material, psychological and social—on which individual and collective human action depends.

The other criticism levelled at Parsons's treatment of values is that he draws a picture of society dominated by general value consensus, and consequently by order, harmony and stability. Parsons in fact recognizes that he has taken the existence of social order as the point of departure for his thinking. But he also insists that in his view order is not an ideal but a *problem*. As it is posed in the Hobbesian tradition, the question of order amounts to asking how society is possible at all—why do men live together in society instead of destroying each other? The philosophers did not, in Parsons's opinion, arrive at any satisfactory answer to this question. He considers the solution reached about the same time by Freud, Durkheim, Mead and Cooley to be the most important discovery of the century in the social sciences. They demonstrated that the basis of social life lies in what Parsons calls the complementarity between the institutionalization of norms and values on the social plane, and the internalization of the same norms and values in individuals. The concurrence of these two processes explains not only the existence of human society but its relative stability. This solution seemed perfectly satisfactory to Parsons, and he made it the cornerstone of his general theory of action.

Various interpretations have been put on this. Parsons has, for example, been accused of saying that the most perfect and desirable social situation would be one in which there was perfect equilibrium between institutionalization and internalization—a state of absolute stability. Nothing, however, justifies this charge. On the contrary, Parsons has often said that such a perfect equilibrium is in practice almost impossible, and more so in complex pluralist societies than in less differentiated ones. In his view, the equation between the social institution and the individual conscience can only be achieved to a certain degree. That degree varies from one person to another, one institution to another and from one society to another.

Similarly, Parsons, has also been charged with saying that all deviance results from 'faulty' socialization. Again, I believe this is a distortion of Parsons's thought. Rather he considers that deviance results from the fact that a perfect coincidence between the institutionalized values and the individual conscience is never achieved. This leaves room for considerable variation in the way and extent to which individual actors internalize the institutionalized culture. And many things happen during socialization which can change its course in innumerable ways and may lead to deviance. What Parsons really finds problematic is not deviance but why in spite of all its hazards socialization is as effective as it generally is—just as it is not conflict which he sees as in need of explanation, but why social order persists in spite of it.

In my opinion, Parsons may be validly criticized, not for having thrown light on the social psychological bases of consensus but for having stopped there and gone no further. There were three directions in which he might have proceeded, but did not. First, he could have explored the whole complex of structural factors in society on which consensus depends and by which it is shored up : the hierarchy of power and authority, economic inequalities, social classes, and many kinds of alienation. Parsons paved the way for such an analysis in his discussions of power and influence, and has sometimes come quite close to carrying it out, but he has never done so.

Second, the analysis of consensus ought to have been complemented by one of conflict. Conflict has not been adequately incorporated into Parsons's model, as critics rightly point out. In social reality there is always stability *and* change, permanence *and* progress, collaboration *and* contention, interdependence *and* obstruction. If this is not apparent in Parsons's sociology, no more is it in the work of those who give pride of place to the analysis of social conflict.

Third, Parsonian sociology takes the existence of norms and values for granted, without asking much about how they originate and evolve. Parsons would perhaps have got round to dealing with this had he pushed his analysis of the cultural system further; of the three principal sub-systems of action—personality, social and cultural systems—the cultural is the most neglected. Paradoxically, the very person who is so often accused of exaggerating the influence of values has made little effort to catalogue them.[23] The result is that in the Parsonian system, culture remains a very static element, whereas the general theory of action ought logically to point to the processes of interaction and exchange through which cultural patterns change.

7.4 The Interest and Limitations of Parsonian Theory

These last remarks lead me in conclusion to some overall criticisms of Talcott Parsons's work, and a brief assessment of what I see as its interest and limitations.

On the credit side of the balance sheet, first of all Parsons made a remarkable effort to build a logical, unified and coherent conceptual scheme for sociology at a very high level of generality. Some people, like adherents of 'radical' sociology, have thought this an intellectually impossible enterprise. But someone had to try it to find out whether it were possible or not. And it is still not certain that the verdict must be negative. In any case, general theory cannot be rejected on grounds of its sterility, as C. Wright Mills wished, when it can be seen how much theoretical and empirical research it has inspired in every direction.

Second, Parsons created a general theoretical framework embracing all the social sciences but distinguishing them from each other and establishing the relationships betwen them without asserting the primacy of any one of them. Certainly, Parsons may be considered over-ambitious in drawing his grand map of the social sciences, and perhaps the results are not up to expectations. But it should be recognized that Parsons's undertaking corresponds to a pressing need of the contemporary social sciences. We have entered an era in which after a period of specialization and fragmentation, social scientists must look for points of contact between their specialist disciplines rather than insist on the differences separating them. Parsons is one of the few sociologists to have scorned the narrow boundaries and extreme specialization of American sociology and, practising what he preaches, to have set out to collaborate with economists, psychologists, anthropologists and political scientists. It is possible that the theoretical framework Parsons developed will not, in the end, prove to be the most suitable basis for interdisciplinary co-operation. It seems to me, however, that his starting point—a theory of action—is valuable, and points the way forward. The idea of action, defined as broadly as it is in Parsons's work, must be the common focus of the social sciences.

Third, Parsons has posed the problem of a theoretically unified sociology in all its aspects. His whole work is a rejection of the idea of piecemeal sociological theories valid for only a limited segment of reality, which Merton calls 'theories of the middle-range'. Parsons has tried in particular to restore theoretical unity between micro-sociology and macro-sociology. He set out to reconcile the American social psychology of Mead, Cooley and Thomas with the macroscopic sociology of Marx, Weber and Pareto. The two traditions had complementary weaknesses. To American sociology, Parsons brought the perspective on total societies which it lacked. To the second tradition Parsons supplied the necessary psychological basis.

Fourth, it must be emphasized that, contrary to what is sometimes said, Parsons has great respect for empirical research. His theory cannot be said to have evolved entirely through logical deduction. He has always been alert to what he could learn from his own research and that of others. Most of the important turning points in the development of his thought have been responses in one way or another to empirical work. What is more, Parsons has often stated his belief in empirical research as the ultimate test of the validity of any theoretical model.

Turning now to the other side of the account, apart from the criticisms of Parsonian theory already listed in this and earlier chapters, the main debits represent the converse of the credits just listed. Parsons had to pay a high price for the unity which he set out to restore within sociology and between the various social sciences. First of all he had to create an analytic model at such a high degree of generality that it lost almost all explanatory power. The Parsonian model is in fact more conceptual than theoretical. It is a vast scaffolding of elaborately arranged categories superimposed one upon another, rather than a real theory capable of supplying an explanation for any set of phenomena. There is very little causality in the Parsonian model, unlike for example the Marxist system of explanation. This is why, on the one hand, it is difficult to make comparisons between the Parsonian model and Marxist theory. On the other hand, because it is more conceptual than causal, the Parsonian model can incorporate several rival explanations, probably including Marxism. Parsons's model provides the sociologist with an intellectual framework enabling him to sort out and organize his observations, which can then be interpreted and explained in various ways. As a result, however, the Parsonian model itself comes to appear like a conceptual scheme empty of all content. There is an important element of truth in George Homans's criticism of Parsons:

> No science can proceed without its system of categories, or conceptual scheme, but this in itself is not enough to give it explanatory power. A conceptual scheme is not a theory. The science also needs a set of general propositions about the relations between the categories, for without such propositions explanation is impossible. No explanation without propositions! But much modern sociological theory seems quite satisfied with itself when it has set up its conceptual scheme.[24]

Second, Parsons has felt obliged to discover the same analytical model, the same four functions, again and again, always and everywhere. These four functions were originally defined by Robert Bales for classifying his observations on the participation of actors in small groups. If it were true, as Bales demonstrated, that these four functions correspond to the fundamental dimensions of the social system of small groups, Parsons believed they ought to be found in any other kind of social system. But to arrive at this conclusion, he had to indulge in considerable flights of imagination and particularly in *analogy by association,* a procedure which ill accords with the logical rigour which Parsons has always sought. What is more, this procedure has often obliged Parsons to impose his scheme on concrete reality, at the risk of bending it to the requirements of the model.

Parsons has too easily taken two postulates for granted: that any system of action contains the four functions of Bales's model, and that the formulation of these four functions is adequate for them to become the main point of the whole vast theory of action. It would have been more reassuring and more in the tradition of scientific research if Parsons had proceeded in a more inductive way. He could, for example, have compared the various ways in which people working in fields other than the sociology of small groups (for example, in the sociology of organizations, industrial sociology or experimental psychology) had defined the functional needs of the systems in which they were interested, and eventually extracted certain common features from them. This was the approach he adopted in *The Structure of Social Action,* in which he put together a theory of action by patiently assembling the pieces from different authors. It is regrettable that he did not follow the same procedure later when he set out to develop his theory further. This would surely have greatly strengthened his theory and set it on much less fragile foundations.

Parsons cut another corner in making use of classical economics, and this too needs to be treated with caution. Following the same logic as when he borrowed Bales's categories, he assumed that analytical concepts useful in economics must also be useful in analysing any system of action. Parsons undeniably made good use of the models of exchange he borrowed from economics. But the result was that the Parsonian system of action, and especially the model of interaction and exchange between sub-systems, always resembles a market or stock exchange in which rather strange 'producers'—the structures and functions of systems of action—assemble to bargain and trade. Again, Parsons has to base this merely on analogies, and they call for the same reservations in this case as in that of the four-function paradigm.

Parsons's theory suffers from a weakness of another kind. It has often been claimed that he over-emphasizes equilibrium, social order and stability. I have already said why I do not concur in this criticism, which only scratches the surface of Parsons's thought and fails to penetrate to the heart of the matter. He deserves criticism more, in my opinion, for not having pursued a dynamic analysis of various contradictions which he himself brought into his system. He introduced a number of potential sources of strain, conflict, and therefore of social change into his model of the system of action. But he has not brought out the existence of these contradictions and the dynamic role they might play. One example is the contradictions inherent in the pattern variables scheme. These are by nature contradictory : universalism is the opposite of particularism, specificity the reverse of diffuseness, and so on. Parsons has neglected the fact that one pole of a variable is never predominant in a concrete system of action to the total exclusion of the other pole. There is always some particularism where universalism is the rule; some affectivity remains where affective neutrality is dominant. In any system of action, the presence of the opposite pole is a latent source of conflict and dispute.

The same goes for the contradiction between 'voluntarism' and functionalism. Several critics have taken Parsons to task for having abandoned the voluntarism of the first version of his theory of action, described in *The Structure of Social Action,* and for having gone over to functionalism. This criticism does not seem to me to be at all well founded. In fact voluntarism has always remained present in the Parsonian system of action—under the name of goal-attainment. In the voluntarist theory of 1937 there was nothing but this function. The criticism I would make is that Parsons has kept only this element of voluntarism and otherwise has completely 'sociologized' the motivation of action. So here again he side-steps the contradictions inherent in systems of action. First, he minimizes the clash between goal-attainment and the counteracting constraints, which stem as much from the functioning of the system itself as from external factors. And secondly, by reducing the motivation of action to learned need-dispositions, he avoids the conflict between instincts and culture, the individual and the social. Recognizing that conflict may be generated within a system of action does not mean that the complementarity of institutionalization and internalization has to be denied; it merely means that this complementarity needs to be examined more deeply. Here I think Parsons has failed to exploit all the possibilities of his system.

If a final verdict has to be passed on Parsons's work, I think it must be judged neither sterile nor devoid of interest. Parsons has, I believe, opened up more possibilities than he himself ventured to explore. So sociological thought will not be advanced by ignoring his contribution. His ideas must be followed up and pushed in new directions. I am convinced that Parsons's systemic model of action holds out numerous opportunities for sociology—including 'radical' sociology—which are only waiting for someone to take the trouble to investigate and make the most of them.

NOTES

1. R. K. Merton, *Social Theory and Social Structure*, enlarged edn (New York, Free Press, 1968); Bernard Barber, *Science and the Social Order* (Glencoe, Ill., Free Press, 1952).

2. Robert N. Bellah, *Tokugawa Religion: The Values of Pre-Industrial Japan* (New York, Free Press, 1957). Bellah gives an account of the stages of this research, carried out under Parsons's supervision, and how he used and adapted various elements of the Parsonian model, in 'Research Chronicle: Tokugawa Religion', in *Sociologists at Work*, edited by P. E. Hammond (New York, Basic Books, 1964).

3. Neil J. Smelser, *Social Change in the Industrial Revolution* (London, Routledge and Kegan Paul, 1959); *The Sociology of Economic Life* (Englewood Cliffs, NJ, Prentice-Hall, 1963).

4. S. M. Lipset, *The First New Nation* (New York, Basic Books, 1963); S. M. Lipset, A. Solari, *et al*, *Elites in Latin America* (New York, Oxford University Press, 1967); Suzanne Keller, *Beyond the Ruling Class: Strategic Elites in Modern Society* (New York, Random House, 1963); Rainer C. Baum, 'Values and Democracy in Imperial Germany', *Sociological Inquiry*, **38** 2, 1969, pp 179–96.

5. Robert Dreeben, *On What is Learned in School* (Reading, Mass, Addison-Wesley, 1968).

6. N. J. Smelser, *Social Change in the Industrial Revolution, op cit*; *Theory of Collective Behaviour* (New York, Free Press, 1962); Chalmers Johnson, *Revolutionary Change* (Boston, Little, Brown and Co, 1966).

7. H. Stuart Hughes, *Consciousness and Society: The Reorientation of European Social Thought, 1890–1930* (New York, Random House, 1958).

8. Perhaps an exception in psychology is James Olds, *The Growth and Structure of Motives* (New York, Free Press, 1955). In anthropology, see Terence S. Turner, 'Parsons's Concept of "Generalized Media of Social Interaction" and its Relevance for Social Anthropology', *Sociological Inquiry* **38** 2, 1968, pp 121–34. Parsons's economic theory seems to be better known to the French than the Americans. See Jean Cuisenier, 'Sur l'action économique', *Revue française de sociologie*, **10** (no. spécial), 1969, pp 575–84, and Alain Caille, 'L'autonomie du système économique, selon Talcott Parsons', *Sociologie du travail*, **12** 2, 1970, pp 190–207.

9. Karl Deutsch, *The Nerves of Government: Models of Political Communication and Control* (New York, Free Press, 1963); 'Integration and the Social System: Implications of Functional Analysis', in *The Integration of Political Communities,* edited by P. E. Jacob and J. V. Toscano (Philadelphia, Lippincott, 1964) pp 179–208.

10. William Mitchell, *Sociological Analysis and Politics: The Theories of Talcott Parsons* (Englewood Cliffs, NJ, Prentice-Hall, 1967).

11. David Easton, *A Systems Analysis of Political Life* (New York, John Wiley, 1964); *A Framework for Political Analysis* (Englewood Cliffs, NJ, Prentice-Hall, 1965).

12. Amitai Etzioni, *Political Unification: A Comparative Study of Leaders and Forces* (New York, Holt, Rinehart and Winston, 1965).

13. C. Wright Mills, *The Sociological Imagination* (New York, Oxford University Press, 1959) especially chapter 2, 'Grand Theory'.

14. Irving Louis Horowitz, 'Social Science, Objectivity and Value-Neutrality: Historical Problems and Projections', *Diogenes* **39**, 1962, pp 17–44; 'Consensus, Conflict and Co-operation: A Sociological Inventory', *Social Forces* **41** 2, 1962, pp 177–88; 'Max Weber and the Spirit of American Sociology', *Sociological Quarterly*, **5**, 1964, pp 344–54. Horowitz is also the historian of the famous 'Project Camelot', in which top American officials and military men attempted to enlist sociologists in a study of the conditions favourable and unfavourable to revolutionary movements in developing countries. See *The Rise and Fall of Project Camelot* (Cambridge, Mass., MIT Press, 1967).

15. Alvin W. Gouldner, *The Coming Crisis of Western Sociology* (New York, Basic Books, 1970). See also Gouldner's collected essays, *For Sociology: Renewal and Critique in Sociology Today* (London, Allen Lane, 1973), including 'Anti-Minotaur: The Myth of a Value-Free Sociology' (pp 3–26), 'The Sociologist as Partisan: Sociology and the Welfare State' (pp 27–68), and 'Some Observations on Systematic Theory, 1945–55' (pp 173–189).

16. Melford E. Spiro, 'A Typology of Functional Analysis', *Explorations* **1**, 1953.

17. At this point, Rocher refers the reader to the discussion of these differences in his *Introduction à la sociologie générale*, vol 2, *L'organisation sociale* (Montreal and Paris, Editions HMH, 1969). English speaking readers may prefer to look at the discussion of systems analysis and functionalism in S. J. Mennell, *Sociological Theory: Uses and Unities* (London, Nelson, 1974), chapter 6. (SJM)

18. Talcott Parsons, 'Some Problems of General Theory in Sociology', in *Theoretical Sociology: Perspectives and Developments,* edited by J. C. McKinney and E. A. Tiryakian (New York, Appleton-Century-Crofts, 1970), pp 35–6. Also see 'Cause and Effect in Sociology', in *Cause and Effect,* edited by Daniel Lerner (New York, Free Press, 1965), pp 51–73.

19. See in particular 'The Position of Sociological Theory', in *Essays in Sociological Theory* (1949 edn only), and *The Social System,* pp 19–22.

20. See especially 'Recent Trends in Structural-Functional Theory' in *Fact and Theory in the Social Sciences,* edited by E. W. Count and G. T. Bowles (Syracuse, Syracuse University Press, 1964), pp 140–53.

21. A. W. Gouldner, *The Coming Crisis of Western Sociology, op cit,* p 331.

22. L. A. Coser, *The Functions of Social Conflict* (New York, Free Press, 1956); *Continuities in the Study of Social Conflict* (New York, Free Press, 1967).

23. Cf. A. W. Gouldner, *The Coming Crisis of Western Sociology, op cit,* p 140. (SJM)

24. *Social Behaviour: Its Elementary Forms* (New York, Harcourt Brace and World, 1961), pp 10–11.

Appendix I.
Bibliography of
Talcott Parsons

1928 ' "Capitalism" in Recent German Literature: Sombart and Weber, I',
Journal of Political Economy, **36** 6, pp 641–61.

1929 ' "Capitalism" in Recent German Literature: Sombart and Weber, II',
Journal of Political Economy, **37** 1, pp 31–51.

1930 Translation of Max Weber, *The Protestant Ethic and the Spirit of Capitalism,* London, Allen and Unwin, and New York, Scribners.

1931 'Wants and Activities in Marshall',
Quarterly Journal of Economics, **46** 1, pp 101–40.

1932 'Economics and Sociology: Marshall in Relation to the Thought of His Time',
Quarterly Journal of Economics, **46** 2, pp 316–47.

1933 'Malthus',
Encyclopedia of the Social Sciences, **10**, pp 68–9.
'Pareto',
Encyclopedia of the Social Sciences, **11**, pp 576–8.

1934 'Some Reflections on "The Nature and Significance of Economics" ',
Quarterly Journal of Economics, **48**, pp 511–45.
'Society',
Encyclopedia of the Social Sciences, **14**, pp 225–31.
'Sociological Elements in Economic Thought, I',
Quarterly Journal of Economics, **49**, pp 414–53.

1935 'Sociological Elements in Economic Thought, II',
Quarterly Journal of Economics, **49**, pp 645–67.
'The Place of Ultimate Values in Sociological Theory',
International Journal of Ethics, **45**, pp 282–316.
'H. M. Robertson on Max Weber and His School',
Journal of Political Economy, **43**, pp 688–96.

1936 'Pareto's Central Analytical Scheme',
Journal of Social Philosophy, **1** 3, pp 244–62.
'On Certain Sociological Elements in Professor Taussig's Thought',
Explorations in Economics: Notes and Essays Contributed in Honor of F. W. Taussig, edited by Jacob Viner, New York, McGraw-Hill, pp 352–79.

1937 *The Structure of Social Action,*
New York, McGraw-Hill. Reprinted by Free Press, New York, 1949.
'Education and the Professions',
International Journal of Ethics, **47**, pp 365–9.

1938 'The Role of Theory in Social Research',
    American Sociological Review, **3**, pp 13–20. (An address delivered before the Annual Institute of the Society for Social Research at the University of Chicago, 1937.)
    'The Role of Ideas in Social Action',
    American Sociological Review, **3**, pp 653–64. (Written for a meeting on the problem of ideologies at the American Sociological Society's annual meeting in Atlantic City, 1937. Reprinted in *Essays in Sociological Theory*.)

1939 'The Professions and Social Structure',
    Social Forces, **17** 4, pp 457–67. (Written to be presented at the annual meeting of the American Sociological Society in Detroit, 1938. Reprinted in *Essays in Sociological Theory*.)
    'Comte',
    Journal of Unified Science, **9**, pp 77–83.

1940 'An Analytical Approach to the Theory of Social Stratification',
    American Journal of Sociology, **45**, pp 841–62. (Reprinted in *Essays in Sociological Theory*.)
    'The Motivation of Economic Activities',
    Canadian Journal of Economics and Political Science, **6**, pp 187–203. (Originally given as a public lecture at the University of Toronto. Reprinted in *Essays in Sociological Theory*, and in *Human Relations in Administration: The Sociology of Organization*, edited by Robert Dubin, 1951.)

1942 'Max Weber and the Contemporary Political Crisis',
    Review of Politics, **4**, pp 61–76, 155–172.
    'The Sociology of Modern Anti-Semitism',
    Jews in a Gentile World, edited by J. Graeber and Stuart Henderson Britt, New York, Macmillan, pp 101–22.
    'Age and Sex in the Social Structure of the United States',
    American Sociological Review, **7**, pp 604–16. (Read at the annual meeting of the American Sociological Society in New York, 1941. Reprinted in *Essays in Sociological Theory*, and in *Sociological Analysis*, edited by Logan Wilson and William Kolb, and in *Personality in Nature, Society and Culture*, edited by Clyde Kluckhohn and Henry A. Murray, first and second edns.)
    'Propaganda and Social Control',
    Psychiatry, **5**, pp 551–72. (Reprinted in *Essays in Sociological Theory*.)
    'Democracy and Social Structure in Pre-Nazi Germany',
    Journal of Legal and Political Sociology, **1**, pp 96–114. (Reprinted in *Essays in Sociological Theory*, revised edn, 1954.)
    'Some Sociological Aspects of the Fascist Movements',
    Social Forces, **21**, pp 138–47. (Written as the Presidential Address to the Eastern Sociological Society at the 1942 meeting. Reprinted in *Essays in Sociological Theory*, revised edn, 1954.)

1943 'The Kinship System of the Contemporary United States',
    American Anthropologist, **45**, pp 22–38. (Reprinted in *Essays in Sociological Theory*.)

1944 'The Theoretical Development of the Sociology of Religion',
Journal of the History of Ideas, **5**, pp 176–90. (Reprinted in *Essays in Sociological Theory*, and in *Ideas in Cultural Perspective*, edited by Philip Wiener and Aaron Noland, New Brunswick, NJ, Rutgers University Press, 1962.)

1945 'The Present Position and Prospects of Systematic Theory in Sociology',
Twentieth Century Sociology, edited by Georges Gurvitch and Wilbert E. Moore, New York, Philosophical Library. (Reprinted in *Essays in Sociological Theory*.)
'The Problem of Controlled Institutional Change: An Essay on Applied Social Science',
Psychiatry, **8**, pp 79–101. (Prepared as an appendix to the Report of the Conference on Germany after the Second World War. Reprinted in *Essays in Sociological Theory*.)
'Racial and Religious Differences as Factors in Group Tensions',
Unity and Difference in the Modern World, edited by Louis Finkelstein *et al*, New York, The Conference on Science, Philosophy and Religion in Their Relation to the Democratic Way of Life, Inc.

1946 'The Science Legislation and the Role of the Social Sciences',
American Sociological Review, **11**, pp 653–66.
'Population and Social Structure',
Japan's Prospect, edited by Douglas G. Haring, Cambridge, Harvard University Press, pp 87–114. (This book was published by the staff of the Harvard School for Overseas Administration. Reprinted in *Essays in Sociological Theory*, revised edn, 1954.)
'Certain Primary Sources and Patterns of Aggression in the Social Structure of the Western World',
Psychiatry, **10**, pp 167–81. (Reprinted in *Essays in Sociological Theory*. Also reprinted as 'The Structure of Group Hostility', in *Crisis and Continuity in World Politics*, 2nd edn, edited by G. Lanyi and W. McWilliams, New York, Random House, 1966, 1973, pp 220–23.)
'Some Aspects of the Relations Between Social Science and Ethics',
Social Science, **22**, pp 213–217. (Read at the annual meeting of the American Association for the Advancement of Science in Boston, 1946.)
'Science Legislation and the Social Sciences',
Bulletin of Atomic Scientists, 1947.
Political Science Quarterly, **62** 2, 1947.
Max Weber: The Theory of Social and Economic Organization.
Co-edited and translated with A. M. Henderson, Oxford University Press. (Reprinted by Free Press, New York, 1957, and Introduction reprinted in *Essays in Sociological Theory*, first edn, 1949.)

1948 'Sociology, 1941–6',
American Journal of Sociology, **53**, pp 245–57. Co-author with Bernard Barber.
'The Position of Sociological Theory',
American Sociological Review, **13**, pp 156–71. (Paper read before the annual meeting of the American Sociological Society, New York City, 1947. Reprinted in *Essays in Sociological Theory*, first edn, 1949.)

1949 *Essays in Sociological Theory Pure and Applied,*
New York, Free Press.
'The Rise and Decline of Economic Man',
Journal of General Education, **4**, pp 47–53.
'Social Classes and Class Conflict in the Light of Recent Sociological Theory',
American Economic Review, **39**, pp 16–26. (Read at the meeting of the American Economic Association in 1948. Reprinted in *Essays in Sociological Theory,* revised edn, 1954.)

1950 'The Prospects of Sociological Theory',
American Sociological Review, **15**, pp 3–16. (Presidential Address read before the annual meeting of the American Sociological Society in New York City, 1949. Reprinted in *Essays in Sociological Theory,* revised edn, 1954.)
'Psychoanalysis and the Social Structure',
The Psychoanalytic Quarterly, **19**, pp 371–84. (The substance of this paper was presented at the meeting of the American Psycho-analytic Association in Washington, DC, 1948. Reprinted in *Essays in Sociological Theory,* revised edn, 1954.)
'The Social Environment of the Educational Process',
Centennial, Washington, DC, American Association for the Advancement of Science, pp 36–40. (Read at the AAAS Centennial Celebration in 1948.)

1951 *The Social System,*
New York, Free Press.
Toward a General Theory of Action.
Cambridge, Harvard University Press. Editor and contributor with Edward A. Shils and others. (Reprinted by Harper Torchbooks, 1962.)
'Graduate Training in Social Relations at Harvard',
Journal of General Education, **5**, pp 149–57.
'Illness and the Role of the Physician: A Sociological Perspective',
American Journal of Orthopsychiatry, **21**, pp 452–60. (Presented at the 1951 annual meeting of the American Orthopsychiatry Association in Detroit. Reprinted in *Personality in Nature, Society, and Culture,* edited by Clyde Kluckhohn, Henry A. Murray, and David M. Schneider, second edn, New York, Knopf, 1953.)

1952 'The Super-ego and the Theory of Social Systems',
Psychiatry, **15**, pp 15–25. (The substance of this paper was read at the meeting of the Psychoanalytic Section of the American Psychiatric Association in Cincinnati, 1951. Reprinted in Parsons, Bales and Shils, *Working Papers in the Theory of Action,* New York, Free Press, 1953 and 1967. Also reprinted in *Social Structure and Personality,* 1964.)
'Religious Perspectives in College Teaching: Sociology and Social Psychology',
Religious Perspectives in College Teaching, edited by Hoxie N. Fairchild, New York, The Ronald Press, pp 286–337.
'A Sociologist Looks at the Legal Profession',
Conference on the Profession of Law and Legal Education, Conference Series Number II, The Law School, University of Chicago,

pp 49–63. (This paper was presented at the first symposium on the occasion of the Fiftieth Anniversary Celebration of the University of Chicago Law School, 1952. Reprinted in *Essays in Sociological Theory,* revised edn, 1954.)

1953 *Working Papers in the Theory of Action,*
In collaboration with Robert F. Bales and Edward A. Shils. New York, Free Press. Re-issued in 1967.

'Psychoanalysis and Social Science with Special Reference to the Oedipus Problem',
Twenty Years of Psychoanalysis, edited by Franz Alexander and Helen Ross, New York, W. W. Norton and Company, pp 186–215. (The substance of this paper was read at the Twentieth Anniversary Celebration of the Institute for Psychoanalysis in Chicago, 1952.)

'A Revised Analytical Approach to the Theory of Social Stratification',
Class, Status and Power: A Reader in Social Stratification, edited by Reinhard Bendix and Seymour M. Lipset, New York, Free Press, pp 92–129. (Reprinted in *Essays in Sociological Theory,* revised edn, 1954.)

'Illness, Theorapy and the Modern Urban American Family',
Journal of Social Issues, **8,** pp 31–44. Co-author with Renée C. Fox. (Reprinted in *Patients, Physicians, and Illness,* edited by E. Gartly Jaco, New York, Free Press, 1958.)

'Some Comments on the State of the General Theory of Action',
American Sociological Review, **18** 6, 1953, pp 618–31.

1954 'The Father Symbol: An Appraisal in the Light of Psychoanalytic and Sociological Theory',
Symbols and Values: An Initial Study, edited by Bryson, Finkelstein, MacIver and McKeon, New York, Harper and Row, pp 523–44. (The substance of this paper was read at the meeting of the American Psychological Association in 1952 in Washington, DC. Reprinted in *Social Structure and Personality.*)

Essays in Sociological Theory (revised edn),
New York, Free Press.

'Psychology and Sociology',
For A Science of Social Man, edited by John P. Gillin, New York, Macmillan, pp 67–102.

'The Incest Taboo in Relation to Social Structure and the Socialization of the Child',
British Journal of Sociology, **5** 2, 1954, pp 101–17.

1955 *Family, Socialization and Interaction Process,*
With Robert F. Bales, James Olds, Morris Zelditch, and Philip E. Slater, New York, Free Press.

' "McCarthyism" and American Social Tension: A Sociologist's View',
Yale Review, Winter, 1955, pp 226–45. Reprinted under title 'Social Strains in America' in *The New American Right* edited by Daniel Bell, New York, Criterion Books, 1955.

1956 *Economy and Society,*
Co-author with Neil J. Smelser. London, Routledge and Kegan Paul, and New York, Free Press.

Éléments pour une theorie de l'action,
With an introduction by François Bourricaud, Paris, Plon.

'A Sociological Approach to the Theory of Organizations',
Administrative Science Quarterly, 1 Part I, June 1956, pp 63–85,
Part II, September 1956, pp 225–39. (Reprinted in *Structure and
Process in Modern Society*, 1960.)

1957 'The Distribution of Power in American Society',
World Politics, 10, October 1957, pp 123–43. (Reprinted in *Struc-
ture and Process in Modern Society*, 1960).
'Malinowski and the Theory of Social Systems',
Man and Culture, edited by Raymond Firth, London, Routledge
and Kegan Paul.
'Man in His Social Environment—As Viewed by Modern Social
Science',
Centennial Review of Arts and Sciences, East Lansing, Michigan
State University, Winter 1957, pp 50–69.
'The Mental Hospital as a Type of Organization',
The Patient and the Mental Hospital, edited by Milton Greenblatt,
Daniel J. Levinson, and Richard H. Williams, New York, Free
Press.
'Réflexions sur les Organisations Réligieuses aux Etats-Unis',
Archives de Sociologie Des Réligions, January–June, pp 21–36.
Sociologia di dittatura,
Bologna, Il Molino.

1958 'Authority, Legitimation, and Political Action',
Authority, edited by C. J. Friedrich, Cambridge, Harvard Univer-
sity Press. (Reprinted in *Structure and Process in Modern Society*.)
'The Definitions of Health and Illness in the Light of American
Values and Social Structure',
Patients, Physicians and Illness, edited by E. Gartly Jaco, New
York, Free Press. (Reprinted in *Social Structure and Personality*.)
'Social Structure and the Development of Personality',
Psychiatry, 21, pp 321–40. (Reprinted in *Social Structure and
Personality*.)
'General Theory in Sociology',
Sociology Today, edited by Robert K. Merton, Leonard Broom and
Leonard S. Cottrell, Jr., New York, Basic Books.
'Some Ingredients of a General Theory of Formal Organization',
Administrative Theory in Education, edited by Andrew W. Halpin,
Chicago, Midwest Administration Center, University of Chicago.
(Reprinted in *Structure and Process in Modern Society*.)
'Some Reflections on the Institutional Framework of Economic Devel-
opment',
The Challenge of Development: A Symposium, Jerusalem: The
Hebrew University. (Reprinted in *Structure and Process in Modern
Society*.)
'Some Trends of Change in American Society: Their Bearing on
Medical Education',
Journal of the American Medical Association, May 1958, pp 31–6.
(Reprinted in *Structure and Process in Modern Society*.)
'The Pattern of Religious Organization in the United States',
Daedalus, Summer 1958, pp 65–85. (Reprinted in *Structure and
Process in Modern Society*.)

'The Concepts of Culture and of Social System',
Co-author with A. L. Kroeber. *American Sociological Review*,
23 5 1958, pp 582–3.

1959 'An Approach to Psychological Theory in Terms of the Theory of
Action',
Psychology: A Study of a Science, vol **3**, edited by Sigmund Koch,
New York, McGraw-Hill, pp 612–711.
'The Principal Structures of Community: A Sociological View',
Community, edited by C. J. Friedrich, New York, Liberal Arts
Press. (Reprinted in *Structure and Process in Modern Society*.)
'*Voting* and the Equilibrium of the American Political System',
American Voting Behavior, edited by Eugene Burdick and Arthur
Brodbeck, New York, Free Press.
'Durkheim's Contribution to the Theory of Integration of Social
Systems',
*Emile Durkheim, 1858–1917: A Collection of Essays, with Trans-
lations and a Bibliography*, edited by Kurt H. Wolff, Columbus,
Ohio State University Press.
'Implications of the Study',
(On Marjorie Fiske's 'Book Selection and Retention in California
Public and School Libraries'.) *The Climate of Book Selection*, a
Symposium of the University of California School of Librarianship.
Berkeley, University of California Press.
'Some Problems Confronting Sociology as a Profession',
American Sociological Review, **24** 4 pp 547–58.
'The School Class as a Social System',
Harvard Educational Review, Fall 1959. (Reprinted in *Social
Structure and Personality*, and in *Education, Economy and Society*,
edited by A. H. Halsey, Jean Floud, and C. Arnold Anderson, New
York, Free Press, 1961.)
'An Approach to the Sociology of Knowledge',
Proceedings, Fourth World Congress of Sociology at Milan, Italy,
September 1959, **4**.

1960 'Mental Illness and "Spiritual Malaise": The Roles of the Psychiatrist
and of the Minister of Religion',
The Ministry and Mental Health, edited by Hans Hofmann, New
York, Association Press. (Reprinted in *Social Structure and Per-
sonality*.)
Structure and Process in Modern Societies
(A collection of essays.) New York, Free Press.
'In memoriam, Clyde Kluckhohn, 1905–1960',
American Sociological Review, **25**, 6 pp 960–2.
'The Mass Media and the Structure of American Society',
Co-author with Winston White. *Journal of Social Issues*, **16** 3
pp 67–77.
'Pattern Variables Revisited: A Response to Professor Dubin's Stimulus',
American Sociological Review, **25** 4, 1960, pp 467–83.
'Toward a Healthy Maturity',
Journal of Health and Human Behavior, Fall 1960. (Reprinted in
Social Structure and Personality.)

'Social Structure and Political Orientation',
World Politics, 13 1, pp 112–28. (A review of S. M. Lipset, Political
Man, and William Kornhauser, The Politics of Mass Society.)
'Review of Reinhard Bendix's Max Weber: An Intellectual Portrait',
American Sociological Review, 25 5 pp 750–2.

1961 'Theories of Society',
Co-editor with Edward Shils, Kaspar D. Naegele and Jesse R. Pitts,
vols 1–2, New York, Free Press.
'Some Principal Characteristics of Industrial Societies',
The Transformation of Russian Society since 1861, edited by C. E.
Black, Cambridge, Harvard University Press. (Reprinted in Struc-
ture and Process in Modern Society.)
'The Link Between Character and Society',
Co-author with Winston White. Culture and Social Character,
edited by S. M. Lipset and Leo Lowenthal, New York, Free Press.
(Reprinted in Social Structure and Personality.)
'The Contribution of Psycho-analysis to the Social Sciences',
Science and Psycho-analysis, 4, 1961.
'The Cultural Background of American Religious Organization',
The Proceedings of the Conference on Science, Philosophy and
Religion, 1960.
'The Point of View of the Author',
The Social Theories of Talcott Parsons, edited by Max Black,
Englewood Cliffs, NJ, Prentice-Hall.
'The Problem of International Community',
International Politics and Foreign Policy, edited by James N.
Rosenau, New York, Free Press.
'Polarization of the World and International Order',
Preventing World War III, edited by Q. Wright, W. M. Evan and
M. Deutsch, New York, Simon and Schuster, 1962. (Also in the
Berkeley Journal of Sociology, 1961.)
'Youth in the Context of American Society',
Daedalus, 91 1, pp 97–123. (Reprinted in Youth: Change and
Challenge, edited by Erik H. Erikson, New York, Basic Books, 1963,
and in Social Structure and Personality.)
'Some Considerations on the Theory of Social Change',
Rural Sociology, 26, 3, pp 219–39.
'A Sociologist's View',
Values and Ideals of American Youth, edited by Eli Ginzberg, New
York, Columbia University Press.
Comment on 'Preface to a Metatheoretical Framework for Sociology',
Llewellyn Gross, American Journal of Sociology, 67 2, pp 136–40.
'In memoriam, Alfred L. Kroeber, 1876–1960',
American Journal of Sociology, 66 6, 616–7.
Comment on 'Images of Man and the Sociology of Religion', by
William Kolb,
Journal for the Scientific Study of Religion, October.
'Discussion of Trends Revealed by the 1960 Census of Population',
Proceedings of the Section on Social Statistics, American Statistical
Association.

1962 Foreword to *Herbert Spencer: The Study of Sociology,*
    Ann Arbor, University of Michigan Press, Ann Arbor Paperback
    Series.
   In memoriam, 'Clyde Kluckhohn, 1905–60'
    (with Evon Z. Vogt), *American Anthropologist,* February 1962.
    (Reprinted as Introduction to a new edition of Kluckhohn's *Navajo
    Witchcraft,* Boston, Beacon Press, 1962.)
   Comment on 'The Oversocialized Conception of Man', by Dennis
    Wrong,
    Psychoanalysis and Psychoanalytic Review, summer.
   Review of *Law and Social Process,* Hurst,
    Journal of the History of Ideas, October–December 1962.
   'The Ageing in American Society',
    Law and Contemporary Problems, Winter 1962.
   'The Law and Social Control',
    Law and Sociology, edited by William M. Evan, New York, Free
    Press.
   In memoriam, 'Richard Henry Tawney, 1880–1962',
    American Sociological Review, **27** 6, pp 880–90.
   Review of *Reason in Society,* Paul Diesing,
    Industrial and Labor Relations Review, July 1963.
   La struttura dell' azione sociale.
    Introduzione di Gianfranco Poggi. Bologna, Il Molino. (Italian
    translation of *The Structure of Social Action.*)

1963 Introduction to Max Weber's *The Sociology of Religion*
    (translated by Ephraim Fischoff from *Wirtschaft und Gesellschaft*),
    Boston, Beacon Press.
   'Social Strains in America: A Postscript (1962)',
    The Radical Right, edited by Daniel Bell, Garden City, New York,
    Doubleday.
   'Christianity and Modern Industrial Society',
    *Sociological Theory, Values, and Sociocultural Change: Essays in
    Honor of Pitirim A. Sorokin,* edited by Edward A. Tiryakian, New
    York, Free Press.
   'Social Change and Medical Organization in the United States',
    Annals of the American Academy of Political and Social Science,
    March 1963.
   'On the Concept of Influence', with rejoinder to comments,
    Public Opinion Quarterly, **27** 1, pp 37–62, 87–92. (Reprinted in
    Sociological Theory and Modern Society.)
   'On the Concept of Political Power',
    Proceedings of the American Philosophical Society, **107** 3, 1963.
    (Reprinted in *Sociological Theory and Modern Society.*)
   'Death in American Society',
    The American Behavioral Scientist, May 1963.

1964 'Some Theoretical Considerations Bearing on the Field of Medical
    Sociology'. Written for a symposium that did not appear,
    Published as chapter 12 of *Social Structure and Personality.*
   Social Structure and Personality,
    A collection of essays. New York, Free Press.

'The Ideas of Systems, Causal Explanation and Cybernetic Control in
Social Science',
Cause and Effect, edited by Daniel Lerner, New York, Free Press,
1965. (Presented at the fourth Hayden Colloquium, Massachusetts
Institute of Technology, 1964.)
'Evolutionary Universals in Society',
American Sociological Review, **29** 3, pp 339–57.
'Max Weber, 1864–1964',
American Sociological Review, April 1964.
'Sociological Theory',
Encyclopedia Britannica, 1965.
'Some Reflections on the Place of Force in Social Process',
Internal War: Basic Problems and Approaches, edited by Harry
Eckstein, New York, Free Press.
'Levels of Organization and the Mediation of Social Interaction',
Sociological Inquiry, Spring 1964.
'Die Jüngsten Entwicklungen in Der Strukturell-Funktionalem Theorie',
Kölner Zeitschrift für Soziologie und Sozialpsychologie, **16** 1, pp
30–49. (English version in Haring *Festschrift.*)
'Youth in the Context of American Society',
Man in a World at Work, edited by Henry Borow, Boston, Hough-
ton Mifflin. (Modified version of an article previously written for
Daedalus, 1961.)
'Evaluation and Objectivity in the Social Sciences: An Interpretation
of Max Weber's Contributions',
An address delivered at the Weber Centennial, April 1964. Pub-
lished in German with discussion in *Max Weber und die Soziologie
Heute,* edited by Otto Stammer, Tubingen, Mohr, 1965. English
version published in the *International Journal of the Social Sciences,*
1965. (Reprinted in *Sociological Theory and Modern Society.*)

1965 'Unity and Diversity in the Modern Intellectual Disciplines: The
Role of the Social Sciences',
Daedalus, **94** 1, pp 39–65.
'An American's Impression of Sociology in the Soviet Union',
American Sociological Review, **30**, 1, pp 121–5.
'Full Citizenship for the Negro American?',
Daedalus, **94** 4, pp 1009–54. (Reprinted in *The Negro American,*
edited by T. Parsons and K. Clark, Boston, Houghton Mifflin,
1966.)

1966 *Societies: Evolutionary and Comparative Perspectives,*
Foundations of Modern Sociology Series, Alex Inkeles (general
editor), Englewood Cliffs, NJ, Prentice-Hall.
'The Political Aspect of Social Structure and Process',
Varieties of Political Theory, edited by David Easton, Englewood
Cliffs, NJ, Prentice-Hall.
The Negro American.
Co-author with Kenneth Clark. Boston, Houghton Mifflin.
'Die Bedeutung der Polarisierung für das Sozialsystem: Die Hautfarbe
als Polarisierungsproblem',
Militanter Humanismus, edited by Alphons Silbermann, Frankfurt,
S. Fischer Verlag.

1967 'The Nature of American Pluralism',
    Religion and Public Education, edited by Theodore Sizer, Boston, Houghton Mifflin.
'Social Science and Theology',
    America and the Future of Theology, edited by William A. Beardslee, Philadelphia, Westminster Press.
Sociological Theory and Modern Society,
    New York, Free Press.
'Death in American Society',
    Essays in Self-Destruction, edited by Edwin Shneidman, New York, Science House.
Comment on Kenneth Boulding's, 'An Economist Looks at the Future of Sociology',
    et al, **1**, 2.

1968 'Components and Types of Formal Organization',
    Comparative Administrative Theory, Preston P. Le Breton, Seattle, University of Washington Press.
Comment on 'The Future of the Nineteenth Century Idea of a University', by Sir Eric Ashby, *Minerva*, Spring 1968.
American Sociology,
    A collection of essays edited by Talcott Parsons. New York, Basic Books.
'Commentary' on Clifford Geertz's, 'Religion as a Cultural System',
    The Religious Situation: 1968, edited by Donald R. Cutler, Boston, Beacon Press.
Christianity.
Emile Durkheim.
Interaction: Social Interaction.
Vilfredo Pareto: Contributions to Economics.
Professions.
Systems Analysis: Social Systems.
Utilitarians: Sociological Thought.
    International Encyclopedia of the Social Sciences, edited by David L. Sills, New York, Macmillan and Free Press.
'The Position of Identity in the General Theory of Action',
    The Self in Social Interaction, edited by Chad Gordon and Kenneth J. Gergen, New York, John Wiley.
The American Academic Profession: A Pilot Study.
    Co-author with Gerald M. Platt, Cambridge, multilith (out of print).
'The Academic System: A Sociologist's View',
    The Public Interest, 13 (special issue).
'On the Concept of Value-Commitments',
    Sociological Inquiry, **38** 2.
'Cooley and the Problem of Internalization',
    Cooley and Sociological Analysis, edited by Albert J. Reiss, Jr, Ann Arbor, University of Michigan Press.
'Sociocultural Pressures and Expectations',
    (A paper presented to the American Psychiatric Association.)
    Psychiatric Research Reports, February.

'Order as a Sociological Problem',
   The Concept of Order, edited by Paul G. Kuntz, Seattle, University of Washington Press.
'The Problem of Polarization on the Axis of Color',
   Color and Race, edited by John Hope Franklin, Boston, Houghton Mifflin.
'Considerations on the American Academic System',
   Co-author with Gerald M. Platt. *Minerva*, **6** 4, pp 497–523.
'Law and Sociology: A Promising Courtship?',
   The Path of the Law from 1967; Harvard Law School Sesquicentennial Papers, edited by Arthur E. Sutherland, Cambridge, Harvard University Press.
'The Disciplines as a Differentiating Force',
   Co-author with Norman Storer. *The Foundations of Access to Knowledge*, edited by Edward B. Montgomery, Syracuse, NY, Syracuse University Division of Summer Sessions.

1969 'Research with Human Subjects and the "Professional Complex"',
   Daedalus, **98** 2, pp 325–60.
   Politics and Social Structure,
   New York, Free Press.
'Review of *Constructing Social Theories*, Arthur L. Stinchcombe',
   Sociological Inquiry, May.

1970 'Some Problems of General Theory in Sociology',
   Theoretical Sociology: Perspectives and Developments, edited by John C. McKinney and Edward A. Tiryakian, New York, Appleton-Century-Crofts.
'Age, Social Structure, and Socialization in Higher Education',
   Co-author with Gerald M. Platt. *Sociology of Education*, **43** 1, pp 1–37.
'Decision-Making in the Academic System: Influence and Power Exchange',
   Co-author with Gerald M. Platt. *The State of the University: Authority and Change*, edited by Carlos E. Kruytbosch and Sheldon L. Messinger, Beverly Hills, Calif., Sage Publications.
'Theory in the Humanities and Sociology',
   Daedalus, **99** 2, pp 495–523.
'The Impact of Technology on Culture and Emerging New Modes of Behaviour',
   International Social Science Journal, **22** 4, pp 607–27.
'Equality and Inequality in Modern Society, or Social Stratification Revisited',
   Sociological Inquiry, **40**, pp 13–72.
'On Building Social System Theory: A Personal History',
   Daedalus, **99** 4, 1970. Reprinted in *The 20th Century Sciences: Studies in the Biography of Ideas*, edited by Gerald Holton, New York, W. W. Norton & Co., 1972.
'Some Considerations on the Comparative Sociology',
   The Social Sciences and the Comparative Study of Educational Systems, edited by Joseph Fischer, Scranton, Pa., International Textbook Company.

1971 *The System of Modern Societies,*
       Englewood Cliffs, NJ, Prentice-Hall, 1971. Companion volume to
       Societies: Evolutionary and Comparative Perspectives (1966).
       'Kinship and the Associational Aspects of Social Structure',
       Kinship and Culture, edited by Francis L. K. Hsu, Chicago, Aldine
       Publishing Company.
       'Comparative Studies and Evolutionary Change',
       Comparative Methods in Sociology, edited by Ivan Vallier, Ber-
       keley, University of California Press, pp 97–139.
       'Evolutionary Universals in Society',
       Essays on Modernization of Underdeveloped Societies, edited by
       A. R. Desai, Bombay, Thacker & Co., Ltd., pp 560–88.
       'The Normal American Family',
       Readings on the Sociology of the Family, edited by Bert N. Adams
       and Thomas Weirath, Chicago, Markham Co., pp 53–66. Re-
       printed from *Man and Civilization: The Family's Search for Sur-
       vival,* by Farber, Mustacchi and Wilson, NY, McGraw-Hill, 1965.
       'Belief, Unbelief and Disbelief',
       *The Culture of Unbelief: Studies and Proceedings from the First
       International Symposium on Belief, Held in Rome, March 22–7,
       1969,* edited by Rocco Caporale and Antonio Grumelli, Berkeley,
       Calif., University of California Press, chapter 12, pp 207–45.

1972 'Higher Education as a Theoretical Focus',
       *Institutions and Social Exchange: The Sociologies of Talcott Par-
       sons and George C. Homans,* edited by Richard Simpson and
       Herman Turk, Indianapolis, Ind., Bobbs-Merrill.
       'Higher Education, Changing Socialization, and Contemporary Stu-
       dent Dissent',
       Co-author with Gerald M. Platt. *Ageing and Society, vol 3: A
       Sociology of Age Stratification,* Matilda W. Riley, Marilyn E.
       Johnson, Anne Foner, and Associates, New York, Russell Sage
       Foundation.
       Readings on Premodern Societies,
       Co-author with Victor Lidz. Englewood Cliffs, NJ, Prentice-Hall.
       'Field Theory and Systems Theory: With Special Reference to the
       Relations Between Psychological and Social Systems',
       *Modern Psychiatry and Clinical Research: Essays in Honor of
       Roy R. Grinker, Sr,* edited by Daniel Offer and Daniel X. Freed-
       man, New York, Basic Books.
       'The School Class as a Social System',
       Socialization and Schools, Reprint Series 1, Compiled from *The
       Harvard Educational Review,* pp 69–90.
       'The Action Frame of Reference and the General Theory of Action
       Systems',
       *Classic Contributions to Social Psychology: Readings with Com-
       mentary,* edited by Edwin P. Hollander and Raymond G. Hunt,
       New York, Oxford University Press, pp 168–76. (Slightly abridged
       from chapter 1 of *The Social System,* Glencoe, Ill., Free Press,
       1951, pp 3–11, 15–19 [*c.* 1951 by Talcott Parsons], with permission
       of the author and Macmillan.)

'The "Gift of Life" and Its Reciprocation',
  Co-author with Renée C. Fox and Victor Lidz. *Social Research*,
  39 3, pp 367–415. Reprinted in *Death in American Experience,*
  edited by Arien Mack, New York, Schocken Books, 1973, pp 1–49.
Review of Reinhard Bendix and Guenther Roth's *Scholarship and
  Partisanship,*
  Contemporary Sociology, **1** 3, pp 200–3.
'Culture and Social System Revisited',
  Social Science Quarterly, **53** 2, pp 253–66. (Reprinted in *The Idea
  of Culture in the Social Sciences*, edited by Louis Schneider and
  Charles Bonjean, Cambridge, England, Cambridge University Press,
  1973, pp 33–46). .
'Commentary on Clark',
  (T.P.'s comment on Terry N. Clark, 'Structural-Functionalism,
  Exchange Theory, and the New Political Economy: Institutionaliza-
  tion as a Theoretical Linkage' (pp 275–98).)
  Sociological Inquiry, **42**, 3–4, pp 299–308.

1973 'Durkheim on Religion Revisited: Another Look at the Elementary
  Forms of the Religious Life',
  Beyond the Classics? Essays in the Scientific Study of Religion,
  edited by Charles Y. Glock and Phillip E. Hammond, New York,
  Harper and Row (Harper Torchbooks), pp 156–180.
The American University
  Co-author with Gerald M. Platt and in collaboration with Neil J.
  Smelser, Cambridge, Mass., Harvard University Press.
'Clyde Kluckhohn and the Integration of Social Science',
  Culture and Life: Essays in Memory of Clyde Kluckhohn, edited
  by Walter W. Taylor, John L. Fischer, and Evon Z. Vogt, Carbon-
  dale, Ill., Southern Illinois University Press, pp 30–57.
Review of W. G. Runciman's *A Critique of Max Weber's Philosophy
  of Social Science,*
  Political Science Quarterly, **88** 2, pp 345–6.
'The Bellah Case, Man and God in Princeton, New Jersey',
  Commonweal, **98** 11, pp 256–9.
'Religious Symbolization and Death',
  Changing Perspectives in the Scientific Study of Religion, edited
  by Allan Eister, New York, Wiley-Interscience.
'Some Reflections on Post-Industrial Society',
  Lecture given to the Japan Sociological Association, 25 November,
  1972. *Japanese Sociological Review*, **24** 2, pp 109–113.
'The Problem of Balancing Rational Efficiency with Communal Solid-
  arity in Modern Society',
  (Memorial Lecture at International Symposium on 'New Problems of
  Advanced Societies' held from 20–4 November 1972, at Keidanren
  Kaikan Tokyo under the sponsorship of Japan Economic Research
  Institute with the support of Ministry of Foreign Affairs.) *Inter-
  national Symposium 'New Problems of Advanced Societies'*, Tokyo,
  Japan Economic Research Institute, pp 9–14.
'The Social Concept of the Present Civilization',
  Tribuna Medica, 25 September, pp 19–20.

Forthcoming

Review of Anthony Giddens' *Capitalism and Modern Social Theory: An Analysis of the Writings of Marx, Durkheim, and Max Weber.* *The American Political Science Review.*

Commentary on Herbert Gintis' 'A Radical Analysis of Welfare Economics',
Quarterly Journal of Economics.

'The University "Bundle": A Study of the Balance Between Differentiation and Integration'.
To appear in Neil Smelser (ed.), *Public Higher Education in California: Growth, Structural Change and Conflict,* Berkeley, Calif., University of California Press.

Social Stratification

Professions
Enciclopedia Italiana, edited by Vincenzo Cappelletti, Rome.

'Sigmund Freud: The Interpretation of Dreams'
To appear in *Daedalus* issue on 'Twentieth-Century Classics Revisited'.

Review of Rene Dubos' *A God Within.*
Commonweal.

Introduction.
For volume by the Commission on the Year 2000, edited by Daniel Bell.

'Some Theoretical Considerations on the Nature and Trends of Change of Ethnicity.'
To appear in *Ethnicity in Our Time,* edited by Nathan Glazer and Daniel P. Moynihan, Boston, Mass., American Academy of Arts and Sciences (Autumn, 1974).

Review of Alvin L. Bertrand's *Social Organization: A General Systems and Role Theory Perspective.*
Social Forces.

'The Present Status of "Structural-Functional" Theory in Sociology.'
To appear in a *Festschrift* for Robert Merton, edited by Lewis Coser.

Comment on J. H. Turner and L. Beghley's 'Current Folklore in the Criticism of Parsonian Action Theory'.
Sociological Inquiry.

Appendix II. Selected Books and Articles on Talcott Parsons

Baum, Rainer C., 'Values and Democracy in Imperial Germany', *Sociological Inquiry*, **38** 2, 1969, pp 179–96.

Bershady, Harold J., *Ideology and Social Knowledge*, Oxford, Basil Blackwell, 1973.

Black, Max (ed), *The Social Theories of Talcott Parsons: A Critical Examination*, Englewood Cliffs, NJ, Prentice-Hall, 1961.

Blain, Robert R., 'A Critique of Parsons's Function Paradigm', *Sociological Quarterly*, **11** 2, 1970, pp 157–68.

Bottomore, T. B., 'Out of this World', *The New York Review of Books*, 6 November 1969.

Caillé, Alain, 'L'autonomie du système économique selon Talcott Parsons', *Sociologie du travail*, **12** 2, 1970, pp 190–207.

Chazel, François, 'Réflexions sur la conception parsonienne du pouvoir et de l'influence', *Revue française de sociologie*, **5** 4, 1964, pp 387–401.

Coleman, James S., 'Comment on "On the Concept of Influence" ', *Public Opinion Quarterly*, **27** 1, 1963, pp 63–82.

Cuisenier, Jean, 'Sur l'action économique', *Revue française de sociologie*, **10** (numéro spécial), 1969, pp 575–84.

Dahrendorf, Ralf, 'Out of Utopia', *American Journal of Sociology*, **64** 2, 1958, 115–27.

Dubin, Robert, 'Parsons's Actor: Continuities in Social Theory', *American Sociological Review*, **25** 4, 1960, pp 457–83.

Fletcher, Ronald, *The Making of Sociology*, vol 3, London, Thomas Nelson, forthcoming.

Friedrichs, Robert W., *A Sociology of Sociology*, New York, Free Press, 1970.

Giddens, Anthony H., ' "Power" in the Recent Writings of Talcott Parsons', *Sociology*, **2** 3, 1968, 257–72.

Gouldner, Alvin W., *The Coming Crisis of Western Sociology*, New York, Basic Books, 1970.

Gregor, A. J., 'Parsons's Functionalism as a Source of Test Hypotheses', *Revue internationale de sociologie*, **5** 3, 1969, pp 160–78.

Jacobs, Harold, 'Aspects of the Political Sociology of Talcott Parsons', *Berkeley Journal of Sociology*, **14**, 1969, pp 58–72.

Lesnoff, M. H., 'Parsons's System Problems', *Sociological Review*, NS **16** 2, 1968, pp 185–215.

Lockwood, David, 'Some Remarks on "The Social System" ', *British Journal of Sociology*, **7** 2, 1956, pp 134–46; and 'Social Integration and System Integration', in *Explorations in Social Change*, edited by G. K. Zollschan and W. Hirsch, London, Routledge and Kegan Paul, 1964.

Loomis, Charles P., *Modern Social Theories: Selected American Writers,* Princeton, NJ, Van Nostrand, 1961.

Mills, C. Wright, *The Sociological Imagination,* New York, Oxford University Press, 1959.

Mitchell, William C., *Sociological Analysis and Politics: The Theories of Talcott Parsons,* Englewood Cliffs, NJ, Prentice-Hall, 1967.

Nisbet, Robert A., *Social Change and History,* New York, Oxford University Press, 1969.

Scott, J. Finley, 'The Changing Foundations of the Parsonian Action Scheme', *American Sociological Review,* **28** 5, 1963, pp 716–35.

Sklair, Leslie, 'The Fate of the "Functional Requisites" in Parsonian Sociology', *British Journal of Sociology,* **21** 1, 1970, pp 30–42.

Sorokin, Pitirim A., *Sociological Theories of Today,* New York, Harper and Row, 1966.

Sprott, W. J. H., 'Principia Sociologica', *British Journal of Sociology,* **3** 3, 1953, pp 203–21; 'Principia Sociologica II', *ibid* **14** 3, 1963, pp 307–20.

Sumpf, Joseph, 'L'approche sociologique du problème du conflict des générations chez Parsons et chez Marx', *Epistémologie sociologique,* **6,** 1968, pp 79–98.

Tausky, C., 'Parsons on Stratification: An Analysis and Critique', *Sociological Quarterly,* **6** 2, 1965, pp 128–38.

Turk, Austin T., 'On the Parsonian Approach to Theory Construction', *Sociological Quarterly,* **8** 1, 1967, pp 37–50.

Turner, J. H. and L. Beghley, 'Current Folklore in the Criticism of Parsonian Action Theory', *Sociological Inquiry,* **43,** forthcoming 1974.

Turner, Terence S., 'Parsons's Concept of "Generalized Media of Social Interaction" and its Relevance for Social Anthropology', *Sociological Inquiry,* **38** 2, 1968, pp 121–34.

Wood, James L., 'The Role of Systematic Theory in Parsons's General Theory of Action: The Case of the Pattern Variables', *Berkeley Journal of Sociology,* **13,** 1968, pp 28–41.

Wrong, Dennis H., 'The Oversocialized Conception of Man in Modern Sociology', *American Sociological Review,* **26** 2, 1961, pp 183–93.